THE POWER OF THE BLOOD OF THE CROSS

A Combined edition of

The Power of the Blood of Jesus
&
The Blood of the Cross

THE
POWER
OF THE
BLOOD
OF THE
CROSS

ANDREW MURRAY

A combined edition of
The Power of the Blood of Jesus
&
The Blood of the Cross

CLC ❖ PUBLICATIONS
Fort Washington, PA 19034

Published by CLC ❖ Publications

U.S.A.
P.O. Box 1449, Fort Washington, PA 19034

GREAT BRITAIN
51 The Dean, Alresford, Hants. SO24 9BJ

AUSTRALIA
P.O. Box 419M, Manunda, QLD 4879

NEW ZEALAND
10 MacArthur Street, Feilding

ISBN 0-87508-691-8

A combined edition of:
The Power of the Blood of Jesus
ISBN 0-87508-381-1
&
The Blood of the Cross
ISBN 0-87508-374-9

This edition 2003

Unless otherwise indicated, Scripture quotations are from
the *New King James Version,* © 1979, 1980, 1982
by Thomas Nelson, Inc. Nashville, Tennessee

This printing 2003

ALL RIGHTS RESERVED

Printed in the United States of America

Book I

The Power of the Blood of Jesus

Preface

A NDREW MURRAY (1828-1917) was a Dutch Reformed
minister. One of four children born to Scottish missionary
Andrew, Sr., and Maria Murray, Andrew Murray had been raised
in what was then considered the most remote corner of the
world—Graaff-Reinet, a wild, rural district in South Africa. It
was to here, after his formal education in Aberdeen, Scotland,
and three years of theological study at Utrecht University in
Holland, that Andrew Murray returned as a missionary and minister.

Murray's first appointment (in 1848) was to a widespread
parish in and around Bloemfontein, in the Orange River Sovereignty, where he labored for eleven years, enjoying the people
and a fruitful ministry. In the midst of this time he spent over a
year in England, convalescing from a severe fever which almost
took his life. Upon his return, he met and married Miss Emma
Rutherfoord of Cape Town. Four years later, in 1860, he accepted a call to Worcester, an important inland town of Cape
Colony.

This was the time of a great revival in America and Wales. It
reached his country, making a great impact on him and his church.
While at Worcester he began the writing of his many devotional
books. Though most were originally in Dutch they were soon
translated into English, and later into many other languages.

In 1864 he took up a pastorate in Cape Town, where he labored for seven years. During this time he served also as national Moderator of his denomination.

In 1871 Mr. Murray accepted a call to a Huguenot community at Wellington, about forty-five miles from Cape Town, where he labored effectively and fruitfully for thirty-five years. In 1874 he founded the Huguenot Seminary (for young ladies) at Wellington, and later a Missionary Training Institute for missionaries to the Kaffirs and other tribes.

Mr. Murray's time was in much demand among the churches of Cape Colony, Orange Free State, Transvaal, and Natal. He insisted that his church permit him to use half of his time in itinerant evangelism. Both in his preaching and his books he laid much emphasis on the deepening of the spiritual life of Christians, which bore abundant fruit.

In 1898, when he was seventy, his old university in Aberdeen conferred upon him the degree of D.D.

The Anglo-Boer War (1899-1902) caused him and his family much heart anguish, having friends and relatives on both sides. He reached out in spiritual concern to the prisoners of war in both camps; the Lord moved mightily among the men and many were converted. Over a hundred of them entered missionary training institutions at the conclusion of the war.

Following Mrs. Murray's death in 1905 he resigned his pastorate at Wellington and devoted his last twelve years to widespread travel, speaking at Keswick, Northfield, and other conventions and evangelistic meetings in England, the United States, Canada, Ireland, Scotland, Holland, and South Africa.

The addresses in this book were published with Mr. Murray's fervent prayer that God would lead all His people into a deeper and more intimate experience of the power of Christ's blood shed on their behalf, without which there can be no freedom of approach to God or truest fellowship with Him.

The Editor

Contents

1

What the Scriptures Teach
About the Blood

"Not without blood"—Hebrews 9:7,18.

GOD has spoken to us in the Scriptures at various times and in different ways, but the voice is ever the same. It is always the Word of the same God.

In light of this, it is important to treat the Bible as a whole and to receive the witness it gives in its various portions concerning certain reiterated truths. By this means we learn to recognize the significance these truths actually occupy in revelation and in the heart of God. Thus, too, we begin to discover what are the foundation truths of the Bible—those which above others demand our attention. Being so prominent in each new aspect of God's revelation, and remaining unchanged when the dispensation changes, they carry an intimation of their spiritual importance.

It is my object in the chapters which follow this introductory one to show what the Scriptures teach us concerning *the glorious power of the blood of Jesus* and the wonderful blessings procured for us by it. I ask my readers to follow me through the Bible and thus see the unique place which is given to *the blood* from the beginning to the end of God's revelation of Himself to man as recorded in the Bible.

· 11 ·

It will become clear that there is no single scriptural idea from Genesis to Revelation more constantly and more prominently in view than that expressed by the words "the blood." Our intent, then, is to see what the Scriptures teach us about the blood—first, in the Old Testament; second, in the teaching of our Lord Jesus Himself; third, in what the apostles taught; and last, what St. John told us of it in the Book of Revelation.

I. What the Old Testament Teaches.

The record about the blood begins at the gates of Eden, but into the unrevealed mysteries of Eden I will not enter. But in connection with the sacrifice of Abel, all is plain. He brought of "the firstlings of his flock" to the Lord as a sacrifice, and there, in connection with the first act of worship recorded in the Bible, blood was shed. We learn from Hebrews 11:4 that it was "by faith" Abel offered an acceptable sacrifice, and his name stands first in the record of those whom the Bible calls "believers." His faith and God's good pleasure in him are closely connected with the sacrificial blood.

In the light of later revelation, this testimony, given at the very beginning of human history, is of deep significance. It shows that there can be no approach to God, no fellowship with Him by faith, and no enjoyment of His favor *apart from the blood*.

Scripture skims rapidly over the following sixteen centuries. Then came the Flood, which was God's judgment on sin by the destruction of mankind. But God brought forth a new earth from that awful deluge of water. Notice, however, that the new earth also had to be baptized with blood. The first recorded act of Noah after he had left the ark was the offering of a burnt sacrifice to God. As with Abel, so with Noah at a new beginning: it was "not without blood."

Sin once again prevailed, and God laid an entirely new foundation for the establishment of His kingdom on earth. By the divine call of Abraham and the miraculous birth of Isaac, God undertook the formation of a people to serve Him. But this purpose was not accomplished apart from *the shedding of the blood.* This is apparent in the most solemn hour of Abraham's life.

God had already entered into a covenant relationship with Abraham; his faith had already been severely tried and he had stood the test. His faith was already reckoned to him for righteousness. Yet he must learn that Isaac, the son of promise, who belonged wholly to God, could be truly surrendered to God only by death. Isaac must die. For Abraham as well as for Isaac, only by death could freedom from the self-life be obtained. Abraham must offer Isaac on the altar.

That was not an arbitrary command of God. It was the revelation of a divine truth: that *only through death can a life be truly consecrated to God.* But it was impossible for Isaac to die and rise again from the dead—for because of sin, death would hold him fast. So his life was spared and a ram was offered in his place. Through the blood that then flowed on Mount Moriah, his life was spared. He and the people which sprang from him live before God "not without blood." By that blood, however, he was spiritually raised again from the dead. The great lesson of substitution is here clearly taught.

Four hundred years pass, and Isaac has become in Egypt the people of Israel. Through her deliverance from Egyptian bondage, Israel was to be recognized as God's firstborn among the nations. Here, also, it is "not without blood." Neither the electing grace of God nor His covenant with Abraham nor the exercise of His omnipotence, which could so easily have destroyed their oppressors, could dispense with the necessity of the blood.

What the blood accomplished on Mount Moriah for one person, who was the father of the nation, must now be experienced by that entire nation. By the sprinkling of the door frames of the Israelites with the blood of the Paschal lamb—by the institution of the Passover as an enduring ordinance with the words "When I see the *blood*, I will pass over you"—the people were taught that life can be obtained only by the death of a substitute. Life was possible for them only through the shed blood of a life given in their place and appropriated by "the sprinkling of that blood."

Fifty days later, this lesson was enforced in a striking manner. Israel had reached Sinai. God had given His law as the foundation of His covenant. That covenant must now be established but, as it is expressly stated in Hebrews 9:7, "*not without blood.*" The sacrificial blood must be sprinkled first on the altar and then on the Book of the Covenant, representing God's side of that covenant; then on the people, with the declaration, "This is the *blood of the covenant*" (Exodus 24).

In that blood the covenant had its foundation and power. It is by the blood *alone* that God and man can be brought into covenant fellowship. That which had been foreshadowed at the gate of Eden, on Mount Ararat, on Moriah, and in Egypt, was now confirmed at the foot of Sinai in a most solemn manner. Without *blood* there could be no access by sinful man to a holy God.

There is, however, a significant difference between the manner of applying the blood in the former cases as compared with the latter. On Moriah the life was redeemed by the shedding of blood on the altar. In Egypt, it was sprinkled on the lintel and door posts of the houses. But at Sinai, it was sprinkled on the *persons themselves*. The contact was closer, the application more powerful.

Immediately after the establishment of the covenant the command was given, "Let them make Me a sanctuary, that I may dwell among them" (Exodus 25:8). They were to enjoy the full blessedness of having the God of the covenant abiding among them. Through His grace they might find Him and then serve

Him in His house.

He Himself gave, with the minutest care, directions for the arrangement and service of that house. But notice that *the blood* is the center and reason of all this. Draw near to the vestibule of the earthly temple of the heavenly King and the first thing visible is the altar of burnt offering, where the shedding of blood continues without ceasing from morning till evening. Enter the Holy Place and the most conspicuous thing is the golden altar of incense, standing in front of the veil, both of which have been sprinkled with blood. Ask what lies beyond the Holy Place and you will be told that it is the Most Holy Place where God dwells. If you ask how He dwells there and how He is approached, you will be told, "Not without blood." The golden ark where His glory shines is itself sprinkled with blood once every year when the high priest alone enters to bring in the blood and to worship God. The highest act in that worship is *the sprinkling of the blood.*

If you inquire further, you will be told that always and for everything *the blood* is the one thing necessary. At the consecration of the tabernacle or of its priests; at the birth of a child; in the deepest penitence on account of sin; in the highest festival; always and in everything the way to fellowship with God is through *the blood alone.*

This continued for fifteen hundred years. At Sinai, in the desert, at Shiloh, in the temple on Mount Moriah it continued— till our Lord came to make an end of all shadows by bringing in the substance and by establishing fellowship with the Holy One in spirit and truth.

II. What Our Lord Jesus Himself Teaches About the Blood.

With Jesus' coming old things passed away, all things became new. He came from the Father in heaven and can tell us in divine words the way to the Father.

It is sometimes said that the words "not without blood" belong to the Old Testament. But what does our Lord Jesus Christ say? Notice, first, that when John the Baptist announced His coming he spoke of Him as filling a dual office. It was first as "the Lamb of God who takes away the sin of the world" and then as "the One who will baptize with the Holy Spirit." The outpouring of the blood of the Lamb of God must take place before the outpouring of the Spirit could occur. Only when all that the Old Testament taught about the blood had been fulfilled could the dispensation of the Spirit begin.

The Lord Jesus Christ Himself plainly declared that His death on the cross was the purpose for which He came into the world, and that it was the necessary condition of the redemption and life which He came to bring. He clearly states that in connection with His death *the shedding of His blood* was necessary.

In the synagogue at Capernaum He spoke of Himself as "the Bread of Life"; of His flesh, that He would "give it for the life of the world." Four times over He said most emphatically, "Unless you eat the flesh of the Son of Man and drink His *blood*, you have no life in you." "Whoever . . . drinks My *blood* has everlasting life." "My *blood* is drink indeed." "He who . . . drinks My *blood* abides in Me, and I in Him" (John 6). Our Lord thus declared the fundamental fact that He Himself, as the Son of the Father, who came to restore to us our lost life, can do this in no other way than by dying for us, by shedding His *blood* for us and then making us partakers of its power.

Our Lord confirmed the teaching of the Old Testament offerings—that man can live only through the death of another, thus obtaining a life that through resurrection has become eternal.

Even Christ Himself cannot make us partakers of that eternal life which He has obtained for us *except* by the shedding of His blood and causing us to drink it. Marvelous fact! *Not without blood* can eternal life be ours.

Equally striking is our Lord's declaration of this same truth on the last night of His earthly life. Before He completed the great work of His life by giving it "as a ransom for many," He instituted the Holy Supper, saying, as He gave them the cup: "This is My blood of the new covenant, which is shed for many for the remission of sins. Drink from it, all of you" (Matthew 26:27–28). "Without shedding of blood there is no remission," and without remission of sins there is no life. But by the shedding of His blood He has obtained a new life for us. By what He calls "the drinking of My blood" He shares His life with us. The blood shed in the atonement—which frees us from the guilt of sin and from death, the punishment of sin—that blood, which by faith we drink, bestows on us His life. The blood He shed was first of all for us and then it is given to us.

III. The Teaching of the Apostles Under the Inspiration of the Holy Spirit.

After His resurrection and ascension our Lord is no longer known by the apostles "after the flesh." Now all that was symbolic has passed away and the deep spiritual truths expressed by those symbols are unveiled. But there is no veiling of the blood. It still occupies a prominent place.

The Epistle to the Hebrews was written purposely to show that the temple service had become unprofitable and was intended by God to pass away now that Christ had come.

Here, if anywhere, it might be expected that the Holy Spirit would emphasize the true spirituality of God's purpose, yet it is just here that "the blood of Jesus" is spoken of in a manner that imparts a new value to the phrase.

We read concerning our Lord that "by His own blood He entered the Most Holy Place" (Hebrews 9:12).

"The blood of Christ . . . shall purge your conscience" (9:14).

"Therefore, brethren, having boldness to enter the Holiest by the blood of Jesus" (10:19).

"You have come . . . to Jesus the Mediator of the new covenant, and to the blood of sprinkling" (12:22–24).

"Jesus also, that He might sanctify the people with His own blood, suffered outside the gate" (13:12–13).

"God . . . brought up our Lord Jesus from the dead, . . . through the blood of the everlasting covenant" (13:20).

By such words the Holy Spirit teaches us that the blood is really the central power in our entire redemption. "Not without blood" is as valid in the New Testament as in the Old.

Nothing but the blood of Jesus, shed in His death for sin, can cover sin on God's side or remove it on ours.

We find the same teaching in the writings of the apostles. Paul writes of "being justified freely by His grace through the redemption that is in Christ Jesus, . . . by His blood, through faith" (Romans 3:24–25), of "having now been justified by His blood" (5:9).

To the Corinthians he declares that the "cup of blessing which we bless, is it not the communion of the blood of Christ?" (1 Corinthians 10:16).

In the Epistle to the Galatians he uses the word "cross" to convey the same meaning, while in Colossians he unites the two words and speaks of "the blood of His cross" (Galatians 6:14; Colossians 1:20).

He reminds the Ephesians that "we have redemption through His blood" and that we "have been made near by the blood of Christ" (Ephesians 1:7 and 2:13).

Peter reminds his readers that they were "elect . . . for obedience and sprinkling of the blood of Jesus Christ" (1 Peter 1:2), that they were redeemed by "the precious blood of Christ" (v. 19).

See how John assured his "little children" that "the blood of Jesus Christ His Son cleanses us from all sin" (1 John 1:7). The Son is He "who came not only by water, but by water and blood" (5:6).

All of them agree in mentioning the blood and in glorying in it—that it is the power by which eternal redemption through Christ is fully accomplished and is then applied by the Holy Spirit.

IV. The Teaching of the Book of Revelation.

But perhaps this is merely earthly language. What has *heaven* to say? What do we learn from the Book of Revelation concerning the future glory and the blood?

It is of the greatest importance to notice that in the revelation which God has given in this book of the glory of His throne and the blessedness of those who surround it, *the blood still retains its remarkably prominent place.*

On the throne John saw "a Lamb as though it had been slain" (Revelation 5:6). As the elders fell down before the Lamb they sang a new song, saying, "You are worthy . . . for You were slain, and have redeemed us to God by Your blood" (vv. 8 and 9).

Later on, when John saw the great company which no man could number, he was told in reply to his question as to who they were: "These are the ones who . . . washed their robes and made them white in the blood of the Lamb" (7:14).

Then again, when he heard the song of victory over the defeat of Satan, its strain was, "They overcame him by the blood of the Lamb" (12:11).

In the glory of heaven as seen by John there was no phrase by which the great purposes of God, the wondrous love of the Son of God, the power of His redemption and the joy and thanksgiving of the redeemed could be gathered up and expressed except this: "The blood of the Lamb." From the beginning to the end of Scripture, from the closing of the gates of Eden to the opening of the gates of the heavenly Zion, there runs through Scripture a golden thread. It is *the blood* that unites the beginning and the end, that gloriously restores what sin had destroyed.

It is not difficult to see what lessons the Lord wishes us to learn from the fact that the blood occupies such a prominent place in Scripture.

(1) *God has no way of dealing with sin or the sinner except through the blood.*

For victory over sin and the deliverance of the sinner, God has no other means or thought than "the blood of Christ." It is indeed something that surpasses all understanding!

All the wonders of grace are focused here: The incarnation, in which Christ took upon Himself our flesh and blood. Love, which spared not itself but surrendered itself to death. Righteousness, which could not forgive sin till the penalty was borne. Substitution, in which the Righteous One atoned for us, the unrighteous. Atonement for sin, making possible the justification of sinners. Renewed fellowship with God. Cleansing and sanctification, to fit us for the enjoyment of that fellowship. True oneness in life with the Lord Jesus. Eternal joy, as expressed in the hymn of praise, "Thou hast redeemed us to God." All these are but rays of the wondrous light which is reflected upon us from "the precious blood of Jesus."

(2) *The blood must have the same place in our hearts which it has with God.*

From the beginning of God's dealings with man, yes, from before the foundation of the world, the heart of God has rejoiced in that blood. Our heart will never rest nor find salvation until we too learn to walk and glory in the power of that blood.

It is not only the penitent sinner longing for pardon who must thus value it. No! — the *redeemed* will experience that just as God in His temple sits upon a throne of grace where the blood is ever in evidence, so there is nothing that draws our hearts nearer to God, filling them with God's love and joy and glory, than living in constant, spiritual view of that blood.

(3) *Let us take time and trouble to learn the full blessing and power of the blood.*

The blood of Jesus is the greatest mystery of eternity, the deepest mystery of the divine wisdom. Let us not imagine that we can easily grasp its meaning. God thought that 4,000 years was necessary to prepare men for it, and we also must *take time* if we are to gain a knowledge of the power of the blood.

Even taking time is of no avail unless there is definite taking of *sacrificial trouble.* Sacrificial blood always meant the offering of a life. The Israelite could not obtain blood for the pardon of his sin unless the life of something that belonged to him was offered in sacrifice. The Lord Jesus did not offer up His life to spare us from the sacrifice of our lives. No, indeed! It was to make the sacrifice of our lives *possible* and *desirable.*

The hidden value of His blood is the spirit of self-sacrifice, for when the blood really touches the heart it works out in that heart a similar spirit of self-sacrifice. We learn to give up ourselves and our lives so as to press into the full power of that new life which the blood has provided.

We give our time in order that we may become acquainted with these things by God's Word. We separate ourselves from sin and worldly-mindedness and self-will so that the power of the blood may not be hindered, for it is just these things that the blood seeks to remove.

We surrender ourselves wholly to God in prayer and faith so as not to think our own thoughts and not to hold our own lives as a prize. We become as those possessing nothing except that which He bestows. Then He reveals to us the glorious and blessed life which has been prepared for us by the blood.

(4) *We can rely upon the Lord Jesus to reveal to us the power of His blood.*

It is by this confident trust in Him that the blessing obtained by the blood becomes ours. We must never in thought separate the blood from the High Priest who shed it and ever lives to apply it.

He who once gave His blood for us will surely, every moment, impart its efficacy. Trust Him to do this. Trust Him to open your eyes and to give you deeper spiritual insight. Trust Him to teach you to think about the blood as God thinks about it. Trust Him to impart to you and to make effective in you all that He enables you to see.

Trust Him above all, in the power of His eternal High Priesthood, to work out in you unceasingly the full merits of His blood so that your whole life may be an uninterrupted abiding in the sanctuary of God's presence.

Believer, you who have come to an understanding of the precious blood, listen to the invitation of your Lord. Come nearer. Let Him teach you; let Him bless you. Let Him cause His blood to become to you spirit and life and power and truth.

Begin now, at once, to open your soul in faith, to receive the full, mighty, heavenly effects of the precious blood in a more glorious manner than you have ever experienced. He Himself will work these things out in your life.

2

Redemption by Blood

"Knowing that you were not redeemed with corruptible things, like silver or gold, from your aimless conduct . . . , but with the precious blood of Christ, as of a lamb without blemish and without spot"—1 Peter 1:18–19.

THE SHEDDING of His blood was the culmination of the sufferings of our Lord. The atoning efficacy of those sufferings was in that shed blood. It is therefore of great importance that the believer should not rest satisfied with the mere acceptance of the blessed truth that he is redeemed by that blood, but should press on to a fuller knowledge of what is meant by that statement and learn what that blood is intended to do in a surrendered soul.

Its effects are manifold, for we read in Scripture of:

Reconciliation through the blood;
Cleansing through the blood;
Sanctification through the blood;
Union with God through the blood;
Victory over Satan through the blood;
Life through the blood.

These are separate blessings but are all included in one sentence: REDEMPTION BY THE BLOOD.

It is only when the believer understands what these blessings are and by what means they become his that he can experience the full power of redemption.

Before passing on to consider in detail these several blessings, let us first inquire in a more general way concerning *the power of the blood of Jesus.*

    I.   Wherein does the power of that blood lie?

   II.   What has that power accomplished?

 III.   How can we experience its effects?

I. Wherein Does the Power of That Blood Lie? or What Is It That Gives to the Blood of Jesus Such Power?

How is it that in the blood there is a power possessed by nothing else?

The answer to this question is found in Leviticus 17:11. "The life of the flesh is in the blood, and I have given it to you upon the altar to make atonement for your souls; for it is the blood that makes atonement for the soul."

It is because the life (or soul) is in the blood, and because the blood is offered to God on the altar, that it has in it redemptive power.

(1) *The soul or life is in the blood*, therefore the value of the blood corresponds to the value of the life that is in it.

The life of a sheep or goat is of less value than the life of an ox, and so the blood of a sheep or a goat in an offering is of less value than the blood of an ox (Leviticus 4:3,13–14, 27–28). But the life of a man is more valuable than that of many sheep or oxen.

And now, who can tell the value or the power of the blood of Jesus? In that blood *dwelt the soul of the holy Son of God.* The eternal life of the Godhead was carried in that blood (Acts 20:28). So the power of that blood in its various effects is nothing less than *the eternal power of God Himself*! What a glorious thought for everyone who desires to experience the full power of the blood.

(2) But the power of the blood lies, above everything else, in the fact that *it is offered to God on the altar for redemption.*

When we think of blood as shed, we think of death; death follows when the blood or the soul is poured out. Death makes us think of sin because death is the punishment for sin. God gave Israel the blood on the altar as the atonement or covering for sin; that means that the sins of the transgressor were laid on the victim and its death was reckoned as punishment for the sins laid upon it.

The blood was thus a life given up to death for the satisfaction of the law of God and in obedience to His command. Sin was so entirely covered and atoned for that it was no longer reckoned as that of the transgressor. He was forgiven.

But all these sacrifices and offerings were only types and shadows till the Lord Jesus came. His blood was the reality to which these types pointed.

Jesus' blood was *in itself* of infinite value because it carried His soul or life. But the atoning virtue of His blood was infinite also *because of the manner in which it was shed.* In holy obedience to the Father's will He subjected Himself to the penalty of the broken law by pouring out His soul unto death. By that death not only was the penalty borne, but the law was satisfied and the Father glorified. His blood atoned for sin and thus made it powerless. Jesus' blood has a marvelous power for removing sin and opening heaven for the sinner, whom it cleanses and sanctifies and makes fit for heaven.

It is because of the wonderful Person whose blood was shed and because of the wonderful way in which it was shed, fulfilling the law of God while satisfying its just demands, that the blood of Jesus has such wonderful power. It is the blood of atonement that has such efficacy to redeem, accomplishing everything for and in the sinner that is necessary for salvation.

II. What Has That Power Accomplished?

As we see something of the wonders that power has accomplished, we shall be encouraged to believe that it can do the same for us. Our intention is to note how the Scriptures glory in the great things which have taken place through the power of the blood of Jesus.

(1) *The blood of Jesus has opened the grave.*

We read in Hebrews 13:20, "Now may the God of peace who brought up our Lord Jesus from the dead, that great Shepherd of the sheep, *through the blood of the everlasting covenant. . . .*"

It was by virtue of the blood that God raised up Jesus from the dead. God's almighty power was not exerted to raise Jesus from the dead *apart from the blood.*

Jesus came to earth as our surety, to become the bearer of the sins of mankind. It was through the shedding of His blood alone that He had the right, as man, to rise again and obtain eternal life through resurrection. His blood had satisfied the law and righteousness of God. By so doing He had overcome the power of sin and brought it to naught. So, also, death was defeated in that its sting, sin, was removed. And the devil also was defeated—he who had the power of death—having now lost all right over Him and us. The blood of Jesus destroyed the power of death, the devil and hell; *His blood has opened the grave.*

He who truly believes this perceives the close connection which exists between the blood and the almighty power of God. It is only through the blood that God exerts His almightiness in dealing with men. Where the blood is, there the resurrection power of God gives entrance into eternal life. The blood has made a complete end of all the power of death and hell; its effects surpass all human thought.

(2) *The blood of Jesus has opened heaven.*

We read in Hebrews 9:12 that Christ "with His own blood . . . entered the Most Holy Place once for all, having obtained eternal redemption."

We know that in the Old Testament tabernacle God's manifested presence was inside the veil. No power of man could remove the necessity for that veil. The High Priest alone could enter there, but only with blood or the loss of his own life. That was a picture of the power of sin in the flesh, which separates us from God. The eternal righteousness of God guarded the entrance to the Most Holy Place so that no flesh might approach Him.

But now our Lord appears, not in a material but in the true temple. As High Priest and representative of His people, He asks for Himself and for sinful children of Adam an entrance into the presence of the Holy One. "That where I am, there they may be also" is His request. He asks that heaven may be opened for each one, even for the greatest sinner who believes in Him. His request is granted. But how is that? It is through *the blood.* He entered with "His own blood." The blood of Jesus has opened heaven.

So it is ever and always through the blood that the throne of grace in heaven remains a settled fact. In the midst of the seven great realities of heaven, listed in Hebrews 12:22–24, the Holy Spirit gives a prominent place to "the blood of sprinkling." In fact, it is placed closer than any other to "God the Judge of all" and "Jesus the Mediator."

It is the constant "speaking" of that blood that keeps heaven open for sinners and sends streams of blessing down to earth. It is through that blood that Jesus, as Mediator, carries on without ceasing His mediatorial work. The throne of grace owes its existence ever and always to the power of that blood.

Oh, the wonderful power of the blood of Christ! Just as it has

broken open the gates of the grave and of hell to let Jesus out—
and us with Him—so it has opened the gates of heaven for Him—
and us with Him—to enter. The blood has an almighty power
over the kingdom of darkness and hell beneath; and over the
kingdom of heaven and its glory above.

(3) *The blood of Jesus is all powerful in the human heart.*

Since it avails so powerfully with God and over Satan, does it
not avail even more powerfully with man, for whose sake it was
actually shed? We may be sure of it. The wonderful power of the
blood is especially manifested on behalf of sinners on earth. Our
text is but one of many places in Scripture where this is emphasized. "You were redeemed from your aimless conduct with the
precious blood of Christ" (1 Peter 1:18–19).

The word "redeemed" has a depth of meaning. It particularly
indicates deliverance from slavery by emancipation or purchase.
The sinner is enslaved under the hostile power of Satan, the curse
of the law, and sin. Now it is proclaimed: "You are redeemed
with the blood, which has paid the debt of guilt and has destroyed the power of Satan, the curse, and sin." Where this proclamation is heard and received, redemption begins in a true
deliverance from a purposeless manner of living and from a life
of sin. The word "redemption" includes everything God does for
a sinner—from the pardon of sin, which it begins with, to the
full deliverance of the body by resurrection (Romans 8:23;
Ephesians 1:14; 4:30).

Those to whom Peter wrote (1 Peter 1:2) were "elect . . . unto
sprinkling of the blood of Jesus Christ." It was the proclamation
about the precious blood that had touched their hearts and
brought them to repentance, awakening faith in them and filling
their souls with life and joy. Each believer was an illustration of
the wonderful power of the blood. Further on, when Peter exhorts them to holiness, it is still the precious blood on which he

bases his plea. On that he would fix their eyes.

Both for the Jew in his self-righteousness and for the heathen in his godlessness, there was only one means of deliverance from the power of sin. It is still the one power that effects daily deliverance for sinners. How could it be otherwise? The blood that availed so powerfully in heaven and over hell is all-powerful also in a sinner's heart. It is impossible for us to think too highly or to expect too much from the power of Jesus' blood.

III. How Does This Power Work?

In what conditions, under what circumstances, can that power secure, unhindered in us, the mighty results it is intended to produce?

(1) The first answer is that, just as it is everywhere in the kingdom of God, *it is through faith.* But faith is largely dependent on knowledge. If knowledge of what the blood can accomplish is imperfect, faith expects little and the more powerful effects of the blood are impossible. Many Christians think that if now, through faith in the blood, they have received assurance of the pardon of their sins, they have a sufficient knowledge of its effects.

So many have no idea that the words of God, like God Himself, are inexhaustible; that they have a wealth of meaning and blessing that surpasses all understanding. They do not realize that when the Holy Spirit speaks of *cleansing through the blood*, such words are only an imperfect human expression of the effects and experiences by which the blood, in an unspeakably glorious manner, will reveal its heavenly life-giving power to the soul. Feeble conceptions of its power prevent in us the deeper and more perfect manifestations of its effects.

As we seek to find out what the Scripture teaches about the blood, we shall see that faith in the blood, *even as we now under-*

stand it, can produce in us greater results than we have yet known; and in the future, a ceaseless blessing may be ours.

Our faith may be strengthened by noticing what the blood has already accomplished. Heaven and hell bear witness to that. Faith will grow by exercising confidence in the fathomless fullness of the promises of God. Let us heartily expect that as we enter more deeply into the fountain, its cleansing, quickening, life-giving power will be revealed more blessedly.

We know that in bathing we enter into the most intimate relationship with the water, giving ourselves up to its cleansing effects. The blood of Jesus is described as a "fountain opened for sin and uncleanness" (Zechariah 13:1). By the power of the Holy Spirit it streams through the heavenly temple. By faith I place myself in closest touch with this heavenly stream; I yield myself to it, I let it cover me and go through me. I bathe in the fountain. It cannot withhold its cleansing and strengthening power. I must in simple faith turn away from what is visible to plunge into that spiritual fountain which represents the Savior's blood, with the assurance that it will manifest its blessed power in me.

So let us with childlike, persevering, expectant faith open our souls to an ever-increasing experience of the wonderful power of the blood.

(2) But there is still another reply to the question as to what else is necessary that the blood may manifest its power.

Scripture connects the blood most closely with the Spirit. It is only where the Spirit works that the power of the blood will be manifested.

THE SPIRIT AND THE BLOOD

We read in the First Epistle of John that "there are three that bear witness on earth: the Spirit, the water, and the blood; and these three agree as one" (1 John 5:8). The water refers to baptism unto repentance and the laying aside of sin. The blood witnesses to redemption in Christ. The Spirit is He who supplies power to the water and the blood. So also are *the Spirit* and *the blood* associated in Hebrews 9:14, where we read, "How much more shall the blood of Christ, who through the eternal Spirit offered Himself without spot to God, purge your conscience . . . ?" It was by the eternal Spirit in our Lord that His blood had its value and power. It is always through the Spirit that the blood possesses its living power in heaven and in the hearts of men.

The blood and *the Spirit* ever bear testimony together. Where the blood is honored in faith or preaching, there the Spirit works; and where He works He always leads souls to the blood. The Holy Spirit could not be given permanently until the blood was shed. This living bond between the Spirit and the blood cannot be broken.

It should be seriously noticed that if the full power of the blood is to be manifested in our souls, we must place ourselves under the teaching of the Holy Spirit. We must firmly believe that He is in us, carrying on His work in our hearts. We must live as those who know that the Spirit of God really dwells within as a seed of life, and He will bring to perfection the hidden, powerful effects of the blood. We must allow Him to lead us.

Through the indwelling of the Spirit the blood will cleanse, sanctify, and unite us to God.

KNOWLEDGE NECESSARY

When the Apostle Peter desired to arouse believers to listen to God's voice with His call to holiness, "Be holy, for I am holy," he reminded them that they had been redeemed by the precious blood of Christ (1 Peter 1:15–19). They needed to know that they had been redeemed and what that redemption signified, but they needed above all to know that "it was not with corruptible things, like silver and gold," things in which there is no power of life, "but with the precious blood of Christ." To have a correct perception of what the preciousness of that blood is—that it provides the power of a perfect redemption—would be to them the basis of a new and holy life.

Beloved Christians, that statement concerns us also. We must *know* that we are redeemed by the precious blood. We must *know* about redemption and the blood before we can experience its power.

In proportion as we more fully understand what redemption is and what the power and preciousness of the blood are, by which redemption has been obtained, we shall the more fully experience its value.

Let us enroll in the School of the Holy Spirit to be led into a deeper knowledge of redemption through the precious blood.

A STRONG DESIRE NEEDED

Two things are necessary. First is a deep sense of need which produces a strong desire to understand the blood better.

The blood has been shed to take away sin. The power of the blood is meant to cancel out the power of sin. We are too easily satisfied with the initial experiences of deliverance from sin. Oh that what remains of sin in us might become unbearable to us! May we no longer be undisturbed by the fact that we, as redeemed ones, sin against God's will in so many things. May the desire for holiness become stronger in us. Should not the thought that the blood has more power than we know of, and can do for us greater things than we have yet experienced, cause our hearts to have this strong desire? If there were more *desire* for deliverance from sin, for holiness and intimate friendship with a holy God, it would be the first impetus for being led further into the knowledge of what the blood can do.

EXPECTATION

The second thing will follow. Desire must become expectation. As we inquire within the Word, in faith, as to what the blood has accomplished, it must be a settled matter with us that the blood can manifest its full power also in us. No sense of unworthiness or of ignorance or of helplessness must cause us to doubt. The blood works in the surrendered soul with a ceaseless power of life.

Surrender yourself to God the Holy Spirit. Fix the eyes of your heart on the blood. Open your whole inner being to its power. The blood on which the throne of grace in heaven is founded can make your heart the temple and throne of God. Take shelter under the ever-continuing sprinkling of the blood. Ask the Lamb of God Himself to make the blood efficacious in you. You will surely experience that there is nothing to compare with the wonder-working power of the blood of Jesus.

3

Reconciliation Through the Blood

"Being justified freely by His grace through the redemption that is in Christ Jesus, whom God set forth to be a propitiation by His blood, through faith"—Romans 3:24–25.

A S WE have seen, several distinct blessings have been procured for us by the power of the blood of Jesus, all of which are included in the one word "redemption." Among these blessings, *reconciliation* takes the first place. God has set forth Jesus to be a propitiation—to provide reconciliation through faith in His blood. Reconciliation with God is first among the things the sinner has to experience if he desires to have a share in redemption. Through it, then, a participation in the other blessings of redemption is made possible.

It is of great importance that the believer who has already received reconciliation should obtain a deeper and more spiritual conception of its meaning and blessedness. If the power of the blood in redemption results in reconciliation with God, then a fuller knowledge of what reconciliation involves is the surest way to obtain a fuller experience of the power of the blood. The heart that is surrendered to the teaching of the Holy Spirit will surely wish to learn what reconciliation involves. May our hearts be opened wide to receive it.

To understand what *reconciliation by the blood* means, let us consider:

I. Sin, which has made reconciliation necessary.
II. God's holiness which foreordained it.
III. The blood of Jesus which obtained it.
IV. The pardon which accompanies it.

I. Sin, Which Made Reconciliation Necessary.

In all the work of Christ, and above all in reconciliation, God's object is the removal and destruction of sin. Understanding about sin is necessary for properly understanding about reconciliation. We must understand what there is about sin that makes reconciliation necessary and how Christ's atonement renders sin powerless. Then faith will have something to take hold of, and the experience of that blessing will be made possible.

Sin has had a twofold effect. It has had an effect on God as well as on man. But the effect it has exercised on God is more terrible and serious! It is because of its effect *on God* that sin has its power *over us*. God, as Lord of all, could not overlook sin. It is His unalterable law that sin must bring forth sorrow and death. When man fell into sin he, by that law of God, was brought under the power of sin. So it is with *the law of God* that redemption must first concern itself. For if sin is powerless against God and the law of God gives sin no authority over us, then its power over us is destroyed. The truth that sin is speechless before God therefore assures us that it no longer has authority over us.

What then was the effect of sin upon God? In His divine nature He ever remains unchanged and unchangeable, but in His relationship and bearing towards man an entire change has taken place. Sin is disobedience, a contempt of the authority of God. It seeks to rob God of His honor as God and Lord. Sin is determined opposition to a holy God. It not only can but *must* awaken His wrath.

While it was God's desire to continue in love and friendship with man, sin has compelled Him to become an opponent. Although the love of God towards men remains unchanged, sin made it impossible for Him to admit man into fellowship with Himself. It has compelled Him to pour out upon man His wrath and curse and punishment, instead of His love. The change which sin has caused in God's relationship to man is awful.

Man is guilty before God. Guilt involves debt. We all know what debt is. It is something that one person can demand from another, a claim which must be met and settled.

When sin is committed, its aftereffects may not be noticed but the *guilt remains.* The sinner is *guilty.* God cannot disregard His own demand that sin must be punished; and His glory, which has been dishonored, must be upheld. As long as the debt is not discharged or the guilt expiated, it is impossible for a holy God to allow the sinner to come into His presence.

We often think that the great question for us is how we can be delivered from the indwelling power of sin, but that is less important than how we can be delivered from *the guilt* which is heaped up *before God.* Can the guilt of our sin be removed? Can the effect of sin *upon God* in awakening His wrath be removed? Can sin be blotted out *before God*? If these things can be done, the power of sin will be broken in us also. It is only through propitiation of God's wrath against sin that the guilt of sin can be removed.

The word translated "propitiation" actually means "an atoning victim." Even unevangelized people had a notion of this concept. But to Israel, God revealed an atonement which could so truly pay for sin and remove its guilt that the original relationship between God and man can be entirely restored. This is *true reconciliation.* The sacrifice must so remove the guilt of sin—that is, the effect of sin on God—that man can draw near to God in the blessed assurance that there is no longer the least guilt resting on him to keep him away from God.

II. The Holiness of God Which Foreordained the Reconciliation.

God's holiness is His infinite, glorious perfection which leads Him always to desire what is good in others as well as in Himself. He bestows and works out what is good in others and hates and condemns all that is opposed to what is good.

In God's holiness His love and wrath are united—His love which bestows itself, and His wrath which casts out and consumes what is evil. It is as *the Holy One* that God ordained atonement in Israel and took up His abode on the mercy seat. It is as *the Holy One* that He, in expectation of New Testament times, said so often, "I am your Redeemer, the Holy One of Israel." It is as *the Holy One* that God wrought out His counsel of reconciliation in Christ.

The wonder of this counsel is that both the holy love and the holy wrath of God find satisfaction in it. Apparently they were in irreconcilable strife with one another. The holy love was unwilling to let man go. In spite of all man's sin, it could not give him up; he must be redeemed. Nor could the holy wrath surrender its demands. The law had been despised; God had been dishonored; God's right must be upheld. There could be no thought of releasing the sinner as long as the law was not satisfied. Obviously, the terrible effect of sin *upon God in heaven* must be counteracted. Somehow the guilt of sin must *justly be removed*, for otherwise no sinner could be delivered. The only solution possible was reconciliation by atonement.

"Atonement" means "covering." It points out that something else has taken over the place where sin was entrenched, so that sin can no longer be seen by God.

But because God is the Holy One and His eyes are as a flame of fire, that which would cover sin must be something of such a nature that it really counteracts the evil that sin has done. It also has to so blot out sin before God that it is really destroyed, and is no longer able to be seen.

Reconciliation for sin can take place only by satisfaction. Satisfaction of the law becomes the basis for reconciliation. And because satisfaction is through a substitute, sin can be punished and the sinner saved. By this means God's holiness also is glorified and its demands met, in addition to the demand of God's love for the redemption of the sinner and the demand of His righteousness for the maintenance of His glory.

We know how this was set forth in the Old Testament laws of the offerings. A clean animal took the place of a guilty man. His sin was laid by confession on the head of the victim, which bore the punishment by surrendering its life unto death. Then the blood—representing a clean life that now, through the bearing of punishment, is freed from guilt—could be brought into God's presence. The blood or life of the animal had borne the punishment in place of the sinner. That blood covered the sinner and his sin, because it had taken his place. It atoned for his sin and provided reconciliation.

Yes, under the Law of Moses there was reconciliation in the *blood.*

But that was not a reality. The blood of cattle or of goats could never truly take away sin; it was only a shadow, a picture, of the *real* atonement. Blood of a totally different character was necessary for an effectual covering of guilt. In accord with the counsel of the holy God, nothing less than the blood of God's own Son could bring about reconciliation. Righteousness demanded it; love offered it. "Being justified freely by His grace through the redemption that is in Christ Jesus, whom God set forth to be a propitiation by His blood"—*here* is reality!

III. The Blood of Jesus Which Brought About the Reconciliation.

Reconciliation requires the satisfaction of the demands of God's holy law.

The Lord Jesus accomplished that. By a willing and perfect

obedience He fulfilled the law under which He had placed Himself. With a spirit of complete surrender to the will of the Father, He bore the curse which the law had pronounced against sin. He rendered, in fullest measure of obedience, all that the law of God could ever ask or desire. The law was perfectly satisfied by Him.

But how can *His* fulfilling of the demands of the law be atonement for the sins of *others*? Because, both through creation and in the holy Covenant of Grace that the Father had made with Him, He was recognized as the head of the human race. Because of this He was able, by becoming flesh, to become a second Adam. When He, the Word, became *flesh*, He placed Himself in a real fellowship with our flesh which was under the power of sin, and He assumed the responsibility for all that sin had done in the flesh against God. His obedience and perfection was not merely that of one man among others, but that of Him who had placed Himself in fellowship with all other men and who had taken their sin upon Himself.

As head of mankind through creation, as their representative in the covenant, He became their surety. As a perfect satisfaction of the demands of the law was accomplished by the shedding of His blood, this atoned for their sin and brought about reconciliation.

Above all, we must never forget that He was God. This bestowed a divine power on Him to unite Himself with His creatures and *to take them up into Himself.* It bestowed on His sufferings the virtue of infinite holiness and power. It made the merit of His blood-shedding more than sufficient to deal with all the guilt of human sin. It made His blood such a *real* propitiation, such *a perfect* covering of sin, that the holiness of God no longer beholds our transgression. It has been, in truth, blotted out. The blood of Jesus, God's Son, has procured a *real, perfect* and *eternal reconciliation.*

What does this mean?

We have spoken of the awful effect of sin on God, of the terrible change which took place in heaven through sin. Instead of favor and friendship and blessing and the life of God bestowed from heaven, man had nothing to look forward to except wrath and curse and death and perdition. He could think of God only with fear and terror, without hope and without love. Sin never ceased to require vengeance; guilt had to be dealt with in full.

But the blood of Jesus, God's Son, has been shed! Atonement for sin has been made! Peace is restored! A change has taken place again, as real and widespread as that which sin had brought about. For those who receive the reconciliation, sin has been brought to nothing! *The wrath of God turns around and hides itself in the depth of divine love.*

The righteousness of God no longer terrifies man. It meets him as a friend with an offer of complete justification. God's countenance beams with pleasure and approval as the penitent sinner draws near to Him, and He invites him into intimate fellowship. He opens for him treasures of blessing. There is nothing now that can separate him from God!

Oh, who can tell the worth of that precious blood!

It is no wonder that mention will be made forever of that blood in the song of the redeemed—that through all eternity, as long as heaven lasts, praise for the blood will resound! "You were slain, and have redeemed us to God by Your blood." How glorious!

But here is the wonder, that the redeemed *on earth* do not more heartily join in that song, and that they are not abounding in praise for the *reconciliation* that the blood has accomplished.

IV. The Pardon Which Accompanies Reconciliation.

That the blood has made atonement for sin by covering it, and that as a result of this such a wonderful change has taken place in the heavenly realms—all this will profit us nothing unless we obtain a personal share in it. It is in the pardon of sin that this takes place.

God has offered a perfect acquittal from all our sin and guilt. Because atonement has been made for sin, we can now be *reconciled* to Him. "God was in Christ reconciling the world to Himself, not imputing their trespasses to them." Following this announcement of reconciliation comes the invitation: "Be reconciled to God." Whoever receives acquittal for sin is reconciled to God! He knows that all his sins are forgiven.

The Scriptures use many different illustrations to emphasize the fullness of forgiveness and to convince the fearful heart of the sinner that the blood has really taken his sin away. "I have blotted out, like a thick cloud, your transgressions, and like a cloud, your sins" (Isaiah 44:22). "You have cast all my sins behind Your back" (Isaiah 38:17). "You will cast all our sins into the depths of the sea" (Micah 7:19). "The iniquity of Israel shall be sought, but there shall be none; and the sins of Judah, but they shall not be found; for I will pardon those whom I preserve" (Jeremiah 50:20).

This is what the New Testament calls justification. It is thus referred to in Romans 3:23–26: "For all have sinned . . . , being justified freely by His grace through the redemption that is in Christ Jesus, whom God set forth to be a propitiation by His blood, through faith, to demonstrate His righteousness, . . . that He might be just and the justifier of the one who has faith in Jesus."

So perfect is the reconciliation, and so truly has sin been covered and blotted out, that he who believes in Christ is looked upon and treated by God as entirely righteous. The acquittal which he has received from God is so complete that there is nothing, absolutely nothing, to prevent him from approaching God with the utmost freedom.

For the enjoyment of this blessedness nothing is necessary except faith in the blood. *The blood alone has done everything!*

The penitent sinner who turns from his sin to God needs only faith in that blood. That is, faith in the power of the blood—that it has truly atoned *for sin* and that it really has atoned *for him.* Through that faith he knows that he is fully reconciled to God and that there is now not the least thing to hinder God from pouring out on him the fullness of His love and blessing.

If he looks toward heaven—which formerly was covered with clouds, black with God's wrath and a coming awful judgment—that cloud is no longer to be seen; everything is bright in the delightful light of God's face and God's love. Faith in the blood manifests in his heart the same wonderworking power that it exercised in heaven. Through faith in the blood he becomes partaker of all the blessings from God which the blood has obtained for him.

Fellow believers, pray earnestly that the Holy Spirit may reveal to you the glory of this reconciliation and the pardon of your sins, made yours through the blood of Jesus. Pray for an enlightened heart to see how completely the accusing and condemning power of your sin has been removed and how God in the fullness of His love and good pleasure has turned towards you. Open your heart to the Holy Spirit that He may reveal in you the glorious effects which the blood has had in heaven. God has set forth *Jesus Christ Himself* to provide reconciliation by His blood! *He is* the propitiation for our sins! *Rely* on Him as having already covered your sin before God! Set Him between yourself and your sins and you will experience how complete the redemption is which He has accomplished and how glorious the reconciliation is through faith in His blood!

Then *through the living Christ* the powerful effects which the blood has exercised in heaven will increasingly be manifested in your heart, and you will know what it means to walk, by the Spirit's grace, in the full light and enjoyment of forgiveness.

And you who have not yet obtained forgiveness of your sins,

does not this work come to you as an urgent call to faith in His blood? Will you allow yourself to be moved by what God has done for you as a sinner? "In this is love, not that we loved God, but that He loved us and sent His Son to be the propitiation for our sins" (1 John 4:10). The precious divine blood has been shed; *atonement is complete*; and the message comes to you, "Be reconciled to God."

If you repent of your sins and desire to be delivered from sin's power and bondage, exercise faith in the blood. Open your heart to the influence of the word that God has sent to be spoken unto you. Open your heart to the message that the blood can deliver you, yes, *even you*, this moment. Only believe it. Say, "That blood is also for me." If you come as a guilty, lost sinner, longing for pardon, you may rest assured that the blood which has already made *a perfect atonement* covers your sin and restores you immediately to the favor and love of God.

So I urge you, exercise faith in the blood. This moment bow down before God and tell Him that you *do* believe in the power of the blood for your own soul. Having said that, stand by it and cling to it. Because of faith in His blood, Jesus Christ will be the covering for *your* sins also.

4

Cleansing Through the Blood

"If we walk in the light as He is in the light, we have fellowship with one another, and the blood of Jesus Christ His Son cleanses us from all sin"—1 John 1:7.

WE HAVE already seen that the most important effect of the blood is reconciliation for sin. Now the fruit of our understanding about the blood and then placing our faith in it for reconciliation is *the pardon of sin.* Pardon is *a declaration of what has already taken place in heaven on the sinner's behalf* and *his hearty acceptance of it.*

This first effect of the blood is not the only one. In proportion as a person, through faith, yields himself to the Spirit of God to understand and enjoy the full power of reconciliation, the blood exerts a further power in the imparting of the other blessings which, in Scripture, are attributed to it.

One of the first results of reconciliation is *cleansing from sin.* Let us see what God's Word has to say about this. Cleansing is often spoken about among us as if it were no more than the pardon of sins or the cleansing from guilt. This, however, is not so. Scripture does not speak of "being cleansed from guilt." Cleansing from sin means deliverance from the *pollution* of sin, not from its guilt. The *guilt* of sin concerns our relationship to God, and our responsibility to make good our misdeeds—or bear punishment for them. The *pollution* of sin, on the other hand, is the sense of defilement and impurity which sin brings to our inner being. It is with *this* that cleansing has to do.

It is of the greatest importance for every believer who desires to enjoy the full salvation which God has provided for him, to understand correctly what the Scriptures teach about this cleansing.

Let us consider:

   I. What the word "cleansing" means in the Old Testament.

  II. What blessing is indicated by that word in the New Testament.

 III. How we may experience the full enjoyment of this blessing.

I. Cleansing in the Old Testament.

In the service of God as ordained by the hand of Moses for Israel, there were two ceremonies to be observed by God's people in preparation for approach to Him. These were the *offerings* or *sacrifices* and the *cleansings* or *purifications*. Both were to be observed, but in different manners. Both were intended to remind man how sinful he was and how unfit to draw near to a holy God. Both were to typify the redemption by which the Lord Jesus Christ would restore to man fellowship with God. As a rule, it is only the offerings which are regarded as typical of redemption through Christ. The Epistle to the Hebrews, however, emphatically mentions the *cleansings* as types: "The tabernacle was . . . symbolic for the present time, in which both gifts and sacrifices are offered . . . *and various washings*" (Hebrews 9:8–10).

If we can imagine the life of an Israelite we shall understand that the consciousness of sin and the need for redemption were awakened both by the cleansings and the offerings.

We must also learn from them what the power of the blood of Jesus actually is.

We may take one of the more important cases of cleansing as

an illustration. If anyone was in a hut or house where a dead body lay, or if he had even touched a dead body or bones, he was unclean for seven days. Death, as the punishment for sin, made everyone who came into association with it unclean. *Cleansing* was accomplished by using the ashes of a young heifer which had been burned, as described in Numbers 19. (Compare Hebrews 9:13–14.) These ashes, mixed with water, were sprinkled by means of a bunch of hyssop on the one who was unclean. He then had to bathe himself in water, after which he was once more ceremonially clean.

The words "unclean," "cleansing," "clean," were used in reference to the healing of leprosy, a disease which might be described as a living death. Read Leviticus, chapters 13 and 14. Here also he who was to be cleansed must bathe in water, having been first sprinkled with water in which the blood of a bird, sacrificially offered, had been mixed. Seven days later he was again sprinkled with sacrificial blood.

An attentive contemplation of the laws of cleansing will teach us that the difference between the cleansings and the offerings was twofold. First, the offerings had definite reference to *transgressions*, for which reconciliation had to be made. Cleansing had more to do with conditions which were not sinful in themselves but were *the result of sin* and therefore must be acknowledged by God's holy people as producing defilement. Second, in the case of an offering, *nothing was done to the offerer himself.* He saw the blood sprinkled on the altar or carried into the Holy Place and he must believe that this procured reconciliation before God. But nothing was done to him. In cleansing, on the other hand, *what happened to the person* was the chief thing. Defilement was something that either through internal disease or outward touch had come upon the man, so the washing or sprinkling with water must take place on himself as ordained by God.

Cleansing was something he could feel and experience. It

brought about a change not only in his relationship to God but in his own condition. In the offering something was done *for* him; by cleansing something was done *in* him. The offering had respect to his *guilt*. The cleansing to the *pollution* of sin.

The same meaning of the words "clean" and "cleansing" is found elsewhere in the Old Testament. David prays in Psalm 51, "*Cleanse* me from my sin," "Purge me with hyssop, and I shall be *clean*." The word used by David here is that which is used most frequently for the cleansing of anyone who had touched a dead body. Hyssop also was used in such cases. David prayed for more than pardon. He confessed that he had been "brought forth in iniquity," that his nature was sinful. He prayed that he might be made pure within. "*Cleanse* me from my sin," was his prayer. He uses the same word later on when he prays, "Create in me a *clean* heart, O God." Cleansing is *more* than pardon.

In the same manner this word is used by Ezekiel, and refers to an inner condition which must be changed. This is evident from chapter 24:11–13 where, speaking of dross being melted from metal, God says, "Because I have purged you, and you were not purged." Later on, speaking of the New Covenant (chapter 36:25), He says, "Then will I sprinkle clean water on you, and you shall be *clean*; I will *cleanse you* from all your filthiness and from all your idols."

Malachi uses the same word, connecting it with fire (chapter 3:3): "He will sit as a refiner and a purifier of silver: he will purify [cleanse] the sons of Levi."

Cleansing by water, by blood, by fire, are all typical of the cleansing which would take place under the New Covenant—an *inner cleansing* and deliverance from the stain of sin.

II. The Blessing Indicated in the New Testament by Cleansing.

Mention is often made in the New Testament of a clean or pure heart. Our Lord said, "Blessed are the *pure* in heart" (Matthew 5:8). Paul speaks of "love from a *pure* heart" (1 Timothy 1:5). Peter exhorts his readers to "love one another fervently with a *pure* heart" (1 Peter 1:22). We read of those who are described as God's people, that God purified (cleansed) their hearts by faith (Acts 15:9). That the purpose of the Lord Jesus concerning those who were His was "to purify for Himself His own special people" (Titus 2:14). As regards ourselves we read, "Let us cleanse *ourselves* from all filthiness of the flesh and spirit" (2 Corinthians 7:11). All these places teach us that cleansing is an inward work wrought in the heart, and that it is subsequent to pardon.

We are told in 1 John 1:7 that "the blood of Jesus Christ His Son *cleanses* us from all sin." This word "cleanses" does not refer to the grace of pardon received at conversion, but to the effect of grace in God's children who walk in the light. We read, "If we walk in the light as He is in the light . . . the blood of Jesus Christ His Son *cleanses* us from all sin." That it refers to something more than pardon appears from what follows in verse 9: "He is faithful and just to forgive us our sins and to *cleanse* us from all unrighteousness." Cleansing is something that comes *after* pardon and is *the result* of it, by the inward and experiential reception of the power of the blood of Jesus in the heart of the believer.

This takes place, according to the Word, first *in the purifying of the conscience*: "How much more shall the blood of Christ . . . *purge* your conscience from dead works to serve the living God" (Hebrews 9:14). The mention already made of the ashes of a heifer sprinkling the unclean typifies a personal experience of the precious blood of Christ. Conscience is not only a judge to give sentence on our actions, it is also the inward voice which bears witness to our relationship to God and to God's relationship to us. When it is cleansed by the blood, then it bears witness that we are well pleasing to God. We receive through the Spirit an inward experience that the blood has so fully delivered us from the guilt and power of sin that we, in our regenerated nature, have escaped entirely from its dominion. Sin still dwells in our flesh with its temptations, but it has no power to rule. The conscience is *cleansed*; there is no need for the least shadow of separation between God and us. We look up to Him in the full power of redemption. The conscience cleansed by the blood bears witness to nothing less than a complete redemption, the fullness of God's good pleasure.

And if the *conscience* is cleansed so also is the *heart*, of which the conscience is the center. We read of having the heart "sprinkled from an evil conscience" (Hebrews 10:22). Not only will the conscience be cleansed but the heart also, including the understanding and the will, with all our thoughts and desires. Through the blood, by the shedding of which Christ delivered Himself up to death and by virtue of which He entered again into heaven, the death and resurrection of Christ are ceaselessly effectual. By this power of His death and resurrection, sinful lusts and dispositions are slain.

"The blood of Jesus Christ cleanses from *all* sin"—from original as well as from actual sin. The blood exercises its spiritual, heavenly power in the soul. The believer in whose life the blood is fully efficacious experiences that the old nature is hindered from manifesting its power. Through the blood, its lusts and desires are subdued and slain and everything is so cleansed that the Spirit can bring forth His glorious fruit. In case of the least stumbling, the soul finds immediate cleansing and restoration. Even unconscious sins are rendered powerless through its efficacy.

We have noted a difference between the *guilt* and the *pollution* of sin. This is of importance for a clear understanding of the matter, but in actual life we must ever remember that they are not thus divided. God through the blood deals with *sin as a whole*. Every true operation of the blood manifests its power simultaneously over the guilt *and* the pollution of sin. Reconciliation and cleansing always go together, and the blood is ceaselessly operative.

Many seem to think that the blood is there so that, if we have sinned again, we can turn again to it to be cleansed. But this is not so. Just as a fountain flows continually and always purifies what is placed in it or under its stream, so it is with this "fountain opened for sin and uncleanness" (Zechariah 13:1). The eternal power of the life of the eternal Spirit works through the blood. Through Him the heart can abide *always* under the flow and cleansing of the blood.

In the Old Testament, cleansing was necessary for each sin. In the New Testament, cleansing depends on Him who ever lives to intercede. When faith sees and desires and lays hold of this fact, the heart can abide *every moment* under the protecting and cleansing power of the blood.

III. How We May Experience the Full Enjoyment of This Blessing.

Everyone who through faith obtains a share in the atoning merit of the blood of Christ has a share *also* in its *cleansing* efficacy. But the experience of its power to cleanse is, for several reasons, sadly imperfect. It is therefore of great importance to understand what the conditions are for the full enjoyment of this glorious blessing.

(1) First of all, *knowledge* is necessary. Many think that pardon of sin is all that we receive through the blood. They ask for and so obtain nothing more.

It is a blessed thing to begin to see that the Holy Spirit of God has a special purpose in making use of different words in Scripture concerning the effects of the blood. Then we begin to inquire about their special meaning. Let everyone who truly longs to know what the Lord desires to teach us by this one word "cleansing" attentively compare all the places in Scripture where the word is used—and where cleansing is spoken of under various synonyms. He will soon feel that there is more promised to the believer than the removal of guilt. He will begin to understand that *cleansing through washing can take away stain.* Although he cannot fully explain in what way this takes place, he will, however, be convinced that he may expect a blessed inward operation of the *cleansing away of the effects of sin* by the blood. Knowledge of this fact is the first condition of experiencing it.

(2) Secondly, there must be *desire.*

It is to be feared that our Christianity is only too pleased to postpone to a future life the experience of the beatitude which our Lord intended for our earthly life: "Blessed are the pure in heart, for they shall see God."

It is not sufficiently recognized that *purity of heart* is a characteristic of *every* child of God, because it is the necessary condition of fellowship with Him and of the enjoyment of His salvation. There is too little inner longing to be really, in all things, at all times, well pleasing to the Lord. Sin and the stain of sin trouble us too little.

God's Word comes to us with the promise of blessing—which ought to awaken all our desires. *Believe* that the blood of Jesus cleanses from all sin. If you learn how to yield yourself up correctly to its operation, it can do great things in you. Should you not every hour desire to experience its glorious cleansing efficacy—to be preserved, in spite of your depraved nature, from the many stains for which your conscience is constantly accusing you? May your desires be awakened to long for this blessing. Put God to the test—to work out in you what He, as the Faithful One, has promised: *cleansing* from all unrighteousness.

(3) The third condition is a *willingness to separate yourself from everything that is unclean.* Through sin, everything in our nature

and in the world is defiled. Cleansing cannot take place where there is not an entire separation from and giving up of everything unclean. "Touch not the unclean thing" is God's command to His chosen ones. I must recognize that all the things surrounding me are unclean.

My friends, my possessions, my spirit, must all be surrendered that I may be *cleansed in each relationship* by the precious blood, and that all the activities of my spirit, soul, and body may experience a thorough cleansing.

He who will keep back anything, however small, cannot obtain the full blessing. He who is willing to pay the full price so as to have his whole being baptized by the blood is on the way to understanding fully this word: "The blood of Jesus cleanses from all sin."

(4) The last condition is *exercising faith in the power of the blood.* It is not as if we, through our faith, bestow upon the blood its efficacy. No, the blood has and ever retains its power and efficacy, but our unbelief closes our hearts and hinders its operation. Faith is simply the removal of that hindrance, the setting open of our hearts for the divine power by which the living Lord will bestow His blood.

Yes, let us believe that there is *cleansing through the blood.*

You have perhaps seen a spring in the midst of a patch of grass. From the much-traveled road that runs by that patch, dust is constantly falling over the grass that grows by the side of the road. But where the water from the spring falls in refreshing and cleansing spray, there is no sign of dust and everything is green and fresh. So the precious blood of Christ carries on its blessed work without ceasing in the soul of the believer who by faith appropriates it. He who by faith commits himself to the Lord and believes that this can and will take place, will experience this.

The heavenly, spiritual effect of the blood can really be experienced every moment. Its power is such that I can always abide in the fountain, always dwell in the wounds of my Lord.

Believer, come, I entreat you; prove how the blood of Jesus can cleanse your heart from all sin.

You know with what joy a weary traveler longs to bathe in a fresh stream, plunging into the water to experience its cooling and cleansing and strengthening effect. Lift up your eyes and see by faith how ceaselessly a stream flows from heaven above to earth beneath. It is the blessed Spirit's influence, through whom the power of the blood of Jesus flows earthwards over souls to heal and to purify them. Oh, place yourself in this stream and simply believe that the words "The blood of Jesus cleanses from all sin" have a divine meaning, deeper, wider than you have ever imagined! Believe that it is the Lord Jesus Himself who will cleanse you in His blood and powerfully fulfill His promise within you. And reckon on the cleansing from sin by His blood as a blessing in which you can confidently abide with daily enjoyment.

5

Sanctification Through the Blood

"Therefore Jesus also, that He might sanctify the people with His own blood, suffered outside the gate"—Hebrews 13:12.

TO A SUPERFICIAL observer it might seem that there is little difference between *cleansing* and *sanctification*, that the two words mean about the same thing. But the difference is great and important.

Cleansing has to do chiefly with the old life and the stain of sin which must be removed, and is only preparatory.

Sanctification concerns the new life and that characteristic of it which must be imparted to it by God. Sanctification, which means union with God, is the distinctive fullness of blessing purchased for us by the blood.

The distinction between these two things is clearly marked in Scripture. Paul reminds us that "Christ loved the church and gave Himself for it, that He might *sanctify* it, having *cleansed* it" (Ephesians 5:25–26, ERV). Having first *cleansed* it, He then *sanctifies* it. Writing to Timothy he says, "Therefore if anyone *cleanses* himself from the latter, he will be a vessel for honor, *sanctified* and useful for the Master" (2 Timothy 2:21). Sanctification is a blessing which follows *after* and *surpasses* cleansing.

This is strikingly illustrated by the ordinances connected with the consecration of the priests, compared with that of the Levites. In the case of the latter, who took a lower position than the priests in the service of the sanctuary, no mention is made of sanctification but the word "cleanse" is used five times (Numbers 8). In the consecration of the priests, on the other hand, the word "sanctify" is often used, because the priests stood in a closer relationship to God than the Levites (Exodus 29; Leviticus 8).

This record at the same time emphasizes the close connection between the sacrificial blood and sanctification. In the case of the consecration of the Levites, reconciliation for sin was made and they were sprinkled with the water of purification for *cleansing*, but they were not sprinkled with blood. But in the consecration of the priests, blood had to be sprinkled upon them. They were *sanctified* by a more personal and intimate application of the blood.

All this was typical of *sanctification through the blood of Jesus,* and this is what we now seek to understand:

    I. What sanctification is.
   II. That it was the great object of the sufferings of Christ.
  III. How it can be obtained through the blood.

I. What Sanctification Is.

To understand what the sanctification of the redeemed is, we must first learn what the holiness of God is. He alone is the *Holy One*. Holiness in the creature must be received from Him.

God's holiness is often spoken of as though it consisted of His hatred against and hostility to sin, but this gives no explanation of what holiness actually is. It is a merely negative statement—that God's holiness cannot bear sin.

Holiness is that attribute of God because of which He always *is* and *wills* and *does* what is supremely good; because of which, also, He desires what is supremely good in His creatures and bestows holiness upon them.

God is called "The Holy One" in Scripture, not only because

He punishes sin but also because He is the Redeemer of His people. It is His holiness, which ever wills what is good for all, that moved Him to redeem sinners. Both the *wrath* of God which punishes sin and the *love* of God which redeems the sinner spring from the same source—His holiness. Holiness is the perfection of God's nature.

Holiness in man is a disposition in entire agreement with that of God, which chooses in all things to will as God wills—as it is written: "As He who called you is holy, you also be holy in all your conduct" (1 Peter 1:15). Holiness in us is nothing other than oneness with God. The sanctification of God's people is effected by *the communication to them of the holiness of God.* There is no other way of obtaining sanctification except by the Holy God bestowing what He alone possesses. He alone is the Holy One. He is the Lord who sanctifies.

By the various meanings which Scripture attaches to the words "sanctification" and "sanctify," a certain relationship with God into which we are brought is pointed out.

The first and simplest meaning of the word "sanctification" is *separation.* That which is taken out of its surroundings by God's command and is set aside or separated as His own possession and for His service—that is holy. This does not mean separation from sin only but from all that is in the world, even from what may be permissible. Thus God sanctified the seventh day. The other days were not unclean, for God saw all that He had made and "indeed it was very good." But only the day which God had taken possession of by His own special act was holy. In the same way God had separated Israel from other nations, and in Israel had separated the priests to be holy unto Him. This separation unto *sanctification* is always God's own work, and so the electing grace of God is often closely connected with sanctification. "You shall be holy to Me, for I the Lord am holy, and have separated you . . . that you should be Mine" (Leviticus 20:26). "You are a holy people to the Lord your God; the Lord your God has chosen you" (Deuteronomy 7:6). God cannot take part with other lords. He must be the sole possessor and ruler of those to whom He reveals and imparts His holiness.

But this separation is not all that is included in the word "sanctification." It is only the indispensable condition for what must follow. When separated, man stands before God in no respect differing from an object without life that has been sanctified to the service of God. If the separation is to be of value, something more must take place. Man must *surrender himself* willingly and heartily to this separation. Sanctification includes *personal consecration* to the Lord to be His.

Sanctification can become ours only when it sends down its roots into and takes its abode in the depths of our personal life—in our will and in our love. God sanctifies no man against his will; therefore a personal, hearty surrender to God is an indispensable part of sanctification.

It is for this reason that the Scriptures not only speak of *God* sanctifying us but they say often that we must sanctify *ourselves.*

But even by consecration, true sanctification is not yet complete. Separation and consecration are together only the preparation for the glorious work that *God will do* as He imparts His own holiness to the soul. "Partaking of the divine nature" is the blessing which is promised to believers in sanctification. "That we may be partakers of His holiness" (Hebrews 12:10) is the glorious aim of God's work in those whom He separates for Himself. But this impartation of His holiness is *not a gift of something that is apart from God Himself.* No! It is only in personal fellowship with Him and partaking of His divine life that sanctification can be obtained.

As the Holy One, God dwelt among the people of Israel to sanctify His people (Exodus 29:45–46). As the Holy One, He today dwells *in* us. It is the presence of God alone that can sanctify. But so surely is this our portion that Scripture does not shrink from speaking of God dwelling in our hearts in such power that we may be "filled with all the fullness of God." *True sanctification* is fellowship with God and His dwelling in us. So it was necessary both that God in Christ should take up His abode in the flesh and that the Holy Spirit should come to dwell in us. This is what "sanctification" means.

II. This Sanctification Was the Object for Which Christ Suffered.

This fact is plainly stated in Hebrews 13:12: "Jesus suffered that He might sanctify His people." In the wisdom of God, a participation in His holiness is the highest destiny of man. Therefore this was the central object of the coming of our Lord Jesus to earth, and above all, of His sufferings and death. It was "that He might sanctify His people" and that they might be "holy and without blame" (Ephesians 1:4).

How the sufferings of Christ attained this end and became *our sanctification* is made plain to us by the words which He spoke to His Father when He was about to allow Himself to be bound as a sacrifice: "For their sakes I sanctify Myself, that they also may be sanctified by the truth" (John 17:19). It was because His sufferings and death were a sanctification of *Himself* that they can become sanctification for *us*.

What does that mean? Jesus was the *Holy One of God*, the Son "whom the Father sanctified and sent into the world," and must He sanctify Himself? He must do so; it was indispensable.

The sanctification which Jesus possessed was not beyond the reach of temptation. In His temptation He needed to maintain it and show how perfectly His will was surrendered to the holiness of God. We have seen that true holiness in man is the perfect oneness of his will with that of God. Through all our Lord's life, from the temptation in the wilderness onwards, He had subjected

His will to the will of His Father and had consecrated Himself as a sacrifice to God. But it was supremely in Gethsemane that He did this. *There* was the hour and the power of darkness, with its temptation to put away the terrible cup of wrath from His lips and to do His own will. It came with almost irresistible power, but He rejected the temptation. He offered up Himself and His will to the will and holiness of God. He sanctified Himself by a perfect oneness of will with that of God. This sanctification of Himself has become the power by which we also may be sanctified through the truth. This is in perfect accord with what we learn from the Epistle to the Hebrews, where, speaking of the words used by Christ, we read, "I have come to do Your will, O God," and then it is added, "By that will we have been sanctified through the offering of the body of Jesus Christ once for all" (Hebrews 10:9–10). It was because the offering of His body was His surrender of Himself to do the will of God that we become sanctified by that will. He sanctified Himself there, for us, that we might be sanctified through the truth. The perfect obedience in which He surrendered Himself that God's holy will might be accomplished in Him was not only the *meritorious cause* of our salvation but is at the same time *the power* by which sin was forever conquered. By the same disposition and the same sanctification it may be created in our hearts.

Elsewhere in this Epistle to the Hebrews the true relationship of our Lord to His own people is even more clearly characterized as having *sanctification* for its chief end. After its speaking of how becoming it was that our Lord should suffer as He did, we read: "For both He who sanctifies and those who are being sanctified are all of one" (Hebrews 2:11). The unity between the Lord Jesus and His people consists in the fact that they both receive their life from one Father and both have a share in *one and the same sanctification.* Jesus is the Sanctifier; they become the sanctified. Sanctification is the bond that unites them. "Therefore Jesus also suffered that He might sanctify His people with His own blood."

If we really desire to understand and experience what sanctification by the blood means, then it is of utmost importance for us first to lay firm hold of the fact that sanctification is the distinguishing feature and purpose of the entire sufferings of our Lord. His sweating of blood (Luke 22:44) was one manifestation of His sufferings. His sanctification of Himself shows the distinctive quality of those sufferings, and therein lay its value and power. Our sanctification is the *purpose* of those sufferings, and only when they attain that purpose do they work out the perfect blessing. In proportion as this is clear to us, we shall press forward into the true meaning and blessing of His sufferings.

It was as the Holy One that God foreordained redemption. It was His will to glorify His holiness in victory over sin by the sanctification of man after His own image. It was with the same object that our Lord Jesus endured and accomplished His sufferings— that we might be consecrated to God. And since the Holy Spirit, the holy God as Spirit, comes into us to reveal in us the redemption that is in Jesus, this continues to be with Him, also, the main object. As the Holy Spirit He is the Spirit of holiness.

Reconciliation, pardon, and cleansing from sin all have an unspeakable value; they all, however, point onwards to *sanctification.* It is God's will that each one who has been marked by the precious blood should know that it is a divine mark, characterizing his entire separation to God. This blood calls him to an undivided consecration—to a life wholly for God—and this blood is the promise and the power of a participation in God's holiness, through which God Himself will make His abiding place in him and be his God.

Oh, that we might understand and believe that "Jesus also suffered that He might sanctify His people with His own blood" (Hebrews 13:12).

III. How Sanctification by the Blood Is Obtained.

An answer to this question in general is that everyone who is a partaker of the virtue of the blood is also a partaker of sanctification and is in God's sight a sanctified person.

In proportion as he lives in close and abiding contact with the blood, he continues to increasingly experience its sanctifying effects, even though he still understands little of how those effects are produced. Let no one think that he must first understand how to lay hold of or explain everything before he may, by faith, pray that the blood might manifest its sanctifying power in him. Not so. It was in connection with the bath of cleansing—the washing of the disciples' feet—that the Lord Jesus said, "What I am doing you do not understand now, but you will know after this." It is the Lord Jesus Himself who sanctifies His people "by His own blood." He who heartily gives himself up to believing worship of and intimate fellowship with the Lamb, who has bought us with His blood, will experience through that blood a sanctification *beyond his conception.* The Lord Jesus will do this for him.

But the believer ought to grow in knowledge also. Only thus can he enter into the full blessing which is prepared for him. We have not only the right but the duty to inquire earnestly what the essential connection is between the blessed effect of the blood and our sanctification—and in what way the Lord Jesus will work out in us, by His blood, those things which we have ascertained to be the chief qualities of sanctification.

We have seen that the beginning of all sanctification is separation to God as His entire possession—*to be at His disposal.* And is not this just what the blood proclaims? The power of sin is broken, we are loosed from its bonds, we are no longer its bondservants; we belong to Him who purchased our freedom with His blood. "You are not your own. For you were bought at a price." This is the language in which the blood tells us that we are God's possession. Because He desires to have us entirely for Himself, He has chosen and bought us and set upon us the distinguishing mark of the blood—as those who are separated from all around them live only for His service. This idea of separation is clearly expressed in the words we so often repeat: "Jesus, that He might sanctify the people with His own blood, suffered outside the gate. Therefore let us go forth to Him, outside the camp, bearing His reproach." "Going out" from all that is of this world was the characteristic of Him who was holy, undefiled, separate from sinners, and it must be the characteristic of all His followers.

Believer, the Lord Jesus *has sanctified you* through His own blood and He desires to make you experience through that blood *the full power* of this sanctification. Endeavor to gain a clear impression of what *has taken place in you* through the sprinkling of that blood. The holy God desires to have you entirely for Himself. No one, nothing, may any longer have the least right over you, *nor have you any right over yourself.* God has separated you unto *Himself,* and that you might feel this He set His mark upon you. That mark is the most wonderful thing that is to be found on earth or in heaven—*the blood of Jesus.* The blood in which the life of the eternal Son of God is, the blood that on the throne of grace is ever before God's face, the blood that assures you of full redemption from the power of sin—that blood is sprinkled upon you as a sign that you belong to God.

Believer, I urge you, let every thought about the blood awaken in you this glorious confession: "By His own blood the Lord Jesus has sanctified me. He has taken complete possession of me for God and I belong entirely to God."

We have seen that sanctification is more than separation. That is only the beginning. We have seen also that personal consecration and hearty and willing surrender to live *only for and in God's holy will* is part of sanctification.

In what way can the blood of Christ work out this surrender in us and make us steadfast in that surrender? The answer is not difficult. It is not enough just to believe in the power of the blood to redeem us and to free us from sin, but we must, above all, notice the *source* of this power.

We know that the blood has this power because of the willingness with which the Lord Jesus surrendered Himself. In the shedding of His blood He sanctified Himself—offered Himself entirely to God and His holiness. It is because of this that the blood is so holy and possesses such sanctifying power. In the blood we have an impressive representation of the utter self-surrender of Christ. The blood ever speaks of the consecration of Jesus to the Father as the Opener of the way and the Supplier of the power for victory over sin. And the closer we come into contact with the blood, and the more we live under the deep impression of having been sprinkled by the blood, the more clearly shall we hear the voice of the blood declaring that "entire surrender to God is the way to full redemption from sin."

The voice of the blood will not speak simply to teach us or to awaken thought; the blood *speaks with a divine and life-giving power*. What it commands, that it bestows. It works out in us the same disposition that was in our Lord Jesus. By His own blood Jesus sanctifies us, that we, holding nothing back, might surrender ourselves with all our hearts to the holy will of God.

But consecration itself, even along with and following separation, is still only a preparation. Entire sanctification takes place *when God takes possession of and fills with His glory the temple that is consecrated to Him.* "There I will meet with the children of Israel, and [they] shall be sanctified by My glory" (Exodus 29:43). Actual complete sanctification consists in God's impartation of His own holiness—*of Himself.*

Here also the blood speaks: it tells us that heaven is opened, that the powers of the heavenly life have come down to earth, that every hindrance has been removed, that God can make His abode with man.

Immediate nearness and fellowship with God are made possible by the blood. The believer who surrenders himself unreservedly to the blood obtains the full assurance that God will bestow Himself wholly and will reveal His holiness in him.

How glorious are the results of such a sanctification! Through the Holy Spirit, the soul has the living experience of God's abiding nearness accompanied by the awakening of the tenderest carefulness against sin, guarded by caution and the fear of God.

But to live in watchfulness against sin does not satisfy the soul. The temple must not only be cleansed but it must be filled with God's glory. All the virtues of divine holiness as manifested in the Lord Jesus are to be sought for and found in this fellowship with God. Sanctification means union with God, fellowship in His will, sharing His life, conformity to His image.

Christians, take note: "Therefore Jesus also . . . suffered outside the gate that He might sanctify the people with His own blood. Let us go forth to Him, outside the camp." Yes, it is *He* who sanctifies His people. "Let us go forth to *Him*." Let us trust *Him* to make known to us the power of the blood. Let us yield ourselves wholly to its blessed efficacy. That blood, through which He sanctified Himself, has entered heaven to open it for us. It can make our hearts also a throne of God, that the grace and glory of God may dwell in us. Yes! "Let us go forth to Him, outside the camp." The one who is willing to give up everything in order that Jesus may sanctify him *will not fail* to obtain the blessing. He who is willing at any cost to experience the full power of the precious blood can confidently reckon that he will be sanctified by Jesus Himself, through that blood.

"May the God of peace Himself sanctify you completely." Amen.

6

Cleansed by the Blood
To Serve the Living God

"Now in Christ Jesus you who once were far off have been made near by the blood of Christ"—Ephesians 2:13.

"How much more shall the blood of Christ . . . purge your conscience . . . to serve the living God?"—Hebrews 9:14.

*S*ANCTIFICATION and *communion with God* are closely related facts in Scripture. Apart from sanctification there can be no such communion. How could one who is unholy have fellowship with a holy God? On the other hand, without communion—intimate converse with God—there can be no growth in holiness. It is always and only in fellowship with the Holy One that holiness can be found.

The close connection between sanctification and communion with God appears plainly in the story of the revolt of Nadab and Abihu. God made this the occasion of a clear statement concerning the peculiar nature of the priesthood in Israel. He said: "I will be sanctified in them that come nigh me" (Leviticus 10:3, KJV). Then again in the conspiracy of Korah against Moses and Aaron—Moses speaking for God said: "Tomorrow morning the Lord will show who is His and who is holy, and will cause him to come near unto Him, even that one whom He chooses He will cause to come near to Him" (Numbers 16:5).

We have already seen that God's election and separation unto Himself of His own are closely bound up with *sanctification*. It is evident here, also, that the glory and blessing secured by this election to holiness is nothing else than *intimate converse with God*. This is indeed the highest, the one perfect blessing for man who was created for God and to enjoy His love. The Psalmist sings: "Blessed is the man whom You choose, and cause to approach You, that he may dwell in Your courts" (Psalm 65:4). In the nature of the case, consecration to God and nearness to Him are the same thing.

The sprinkling of the blood which sanctifies man unto God and takes possession of him for God, bestows, at the same time, the right of *communion with God*.

It was thus with the priest in Israel. In the record of their consecration we read: "Then he brought Aaron's sons. And Moses put some of the blood on the tips of their right ears, on the thumbs of their right hands, and on the big toes of their right feet" (Leviticus 8:24). Those who belong to God may, and indeed *must*, live in nearness to Him; they belong to Him. This is illustrated in the case of our Lord, our Great High Priest, who "*with His own blood* entered the Most Holy Place once for all." It is the same with every believer, according to the Word: "Therefore, brethren, having boldness to enter the Holiest *by the blood of Jesus*, . . . *let us draw near*, . . . having our hearts sprinkled from an evil conscience" (Hebrews 10:19–22). The word "enter" as used in this verse is the peculiar word used of the approach of the priest to God. In the same way in the Book of Revelation, our right to draw near as priests is declared to be by the *power of the blood*. "*You* have redeemed us to God by Your blood . . . and have made us kings and priests to our God" (Revelation 5:9–10). "These are the ones who . . . washed their robes and made them white *in the blood of the Lamb*. Therefore they are before the throne of God, and serve Him day and night in His temple" (Revelation 7:14–15).

One of the most glorious blessings made possible for us by the power of the blood is that of drawing near the throne, into the very presence of God. That we may understand what this blessing means, let us consider what is contained in it. It includes:

    I.   The right to dwell in the presence of God.

    II. The ministry of offering spiritual sacrifices to God.

    III. The power to obtain blessing for others.

I. The Right to Dwell in the Presence of God.

Although this privilege belonged exclusively to the priests in Israel, we know that *they* had free access to the dwelling place of God. They had to abide there continually. As members of the household of God they ate the showbread and partook of the sacrifices. A true Israelite realized there was no higher privilege than this. It is thus expressed by the Psalmist: "Blessed"—or happy—"is the man whom You choose, and cause to approach You, that he may dwell in Your courts. We shall be satisfied with the goodness of Your house, of Your holy temple" (Psalm 65:4).

It was because of the manifested presence of God there that believers in those old days longed after the house of God with such strong desire. The cry was, "When shall I come and appear before God?" (Psalm 42:2). They understood something of the spiritual meaning of the privilege of "drawing near to God." It represented to them the enjoyment of His love and fellowship and protection and blessing. They could exclaim, "Oh, how great is Your goodness, which You have laid up for those who fear You. . . . You shall hide them in the secret place of Your presence" (Psalm 31:19–20).

The precious blood of Christ has opened the way for the believer into God's presence; and *intimate converse* with Him is a deep, spiritual reality. He who knows the full power of the blood is brought so near that he can always live in the immediate presence of God and in the enjoyment of the unspeakable blessings attached to it. There the child of God has the assurance of God's love; he experiences and enjoys it. God Himself imparts it. He lives daily in the friendship and fellowship of God. As God's child he makes known his thoughts and wishes to the Father with perfect freedom. In this communion with God he possesses all that he needs; he lacks no good thing. His soul is kept in perfect rest and peace because God is with him. He receives all requisite direction and teaching. God's eye is ever upon him, guiding him. In communion with God he is able to hear the softest whispers of the Holy Spirit. He learns to understand the slightest sign of his Father's will and to follow it. His strength continually increases, for God is his strength and God is ever with him.

Fellowship with God exercises a wonderful influence on his life and character. The holy presence of God fills him with humility and fear and circumspection. He lives as in the presence of a king. Fellowship with God produces in him godlike attitudes. Beholding the image of God, he is changed into the same image. Dwelling with the Holy One makes him holy. He can say, "It is good for me to draw near to God" (Psalm 73:28).

O you who are the children of the New Covenant, have not you a thousand times more reason to speak thus, now that the veil has been rent asunder and the way opened for living always in God's holy presence? May this high privilege awaken our desires. Communion with God, fellowship with God, dwelling with God and He with us makes it impossible for us to be satisfied with anything less. This is the true Christian life.

But communion with God is not only so blessed because of the *salvation* enjoyed in it but also on account of the *service* that may be rendered because of that intimate converse.

Let us therefore consider:

II. The Ministry of Offering Spiritual Sacrifices to God.

Our divine calling to bring to God spiritual sacrifices is a great privilege. The personal enjoyment that the priests experienced in drawing near to God was of less importance than this grand fact. They were appointed as *servants* of the Holy Place, to bring to God in His house that which belonged to Him. Even so, only as they also found joy in drawing near to God could that service become truly blessed.

The priestly service consisted of: the bringing in of the blood of sprinkling, the preparation of the incense to fill the house with its fragrance, and the ordering of everything that pertained to the arrangement of His house. It was required that they so guard and serve and provide for the dwelling place of the Most High that it should be worthy of Him and of His glory, and that His good pleasure in it might be satisfied.

If the blood of Jesus brings *us* near, it is also chiefly that we should live before God *as His servants* and bring to Him the spiritual sacrifices which are well pleasing in His sight.

The priests brought the blood into the Holy Place before God. In *our* communion with God there is no offering that we can bring more pleasing to Him than a believing honoring of the blood of the Lamb. Every act of humble trust or of hearty thanksgiving in which we direct the attention of the Father to the blood and speak its praises is acceptable to Him. Our whole abiding there in communion with God, from hour to hour, must be a glorifying of *the blood* before God.

The priests brought *the incense* into the Holy Place, so as to fill God's house with fragrance. The prayers of God's people are the delightful incense with which He desires to be surrounded in His habitation. The value of prayer does not consist merely in its being the means of obtaining things *we* need. No, it has a higher aim than that! It is a ministry of God in which *He delights.*

The life of a believer who truly enjoys drawing near to God through the blood is a life of unceasing prayer. In a deep sense of dependence for each moment, for each step, grace is sought for and expected. In the blessed conviction of God's nearness and unchanging goodness, the soul pours itself out in the confident assurance of faith that every promise will be fulfilled. In the midst of the joy which the light of God's face bestows, there arises at the same time along with prayer, thanksgiving and adoration.

These are the spiritual offerings—the offerings of the lips of the priests of God, continually presented to Him—from those who have been *sanctified and brought near by the blood* that they might ever live and walk in His presence.

But there is still something more. It was the duty of the Levitical priests to attend to every stipulation for cleansing or provision that was necessary in the ministry of the temple. What is the required ministry now under the New Covenant? Thanks be to God, there *are* no essential outward arrangements for divine worship. No! The Father has so ordered that whatever anyone does who is walking in His presence—just because of that, it becomes a spiritual offering. Everything the believer does, if only he does it as in God's presence and inspired by the priestly attitude which offers it to God as a service, is a priestly sacrifice, well pleasing to God. "Therefore, whether you eat or drink, or whatever you do, do all to the glory of God" (1 Corinthians 10:31). "And whatever you do in word or deed, do all in the name of the Lord Jesus, giving thanks to God the Father through Him" (Colossians 3:17). In this way, all our actions become thank offerings to God. How little Christians recognize the glory of a life of complete consecration, to be spent always in close fellowship with God!

Cleansed, *sanctified*, and *brought near*, by the power of the blood, the result is that my earthly calling, my whole life, even my eating and drinking are a spiritual service. My work, my business, my money, my house, everything with which I have to do becomes sanctified by the presence of God because I myself walk in His presence. The poorest earthly work is a priestly service because it is performed by *a priest of God's temple*.

But even *this* does not exhaust the glory of the blessing of communion with God. The highest blessing of the priesthood is that the priest appears before God as *the representative of others.*

III. The Power to Obtain Blessing for Others Is What Gives Nearness to God Its Full Glory.

In Israel the priests were the mediators between God and the people. They carried into the presence of God the sins and needs of the people. They obtained from God the power to declare the pardon of sin and the right of blessing the people.

This privilege now belongs to *all believers* as the priestly family of the New Covenant. God permits His redeemed ones to approach Him through Christ's blood in order that He might bless them so that they may become a blessing to others. Let us exercise our priestly privileges. Priestly mediation, a priestly heart that can have the needed sympathy for those who are weak, a priestly power to obtain the blessing of God in the temple and convey it to others—how wonderful these things are! In *them* intimate communion—the drawing near to God through the blood—manifests its highest power and glory.

We can exercise our priestly dignity in a twofold manner:

(1) *By intercession.*

The ministry of intercession is one of the highest privileges of the child of God. It does not mean that in this ministry we, having ascertained that there is a need in the world or in some particular person, pour out our wishes in prayer to God asking for the necessary supply. That is good so far as it goes, and brings a blessing with it. But the peculiar ministry of intercession is something more wonderful than that and finds its power in "the prayer of faith." This "prayer of faith" is a different thing from the outpouring of our wishes to God and leaving them with Him.

In the true "prayer of faith" the intercessor must spend time with God to appropriate the promises of His Word and must permit himself to be taught by the Holy Spirit whether the promises can be applied to this particular case. He takes upon himself, as a burden, the sin and need which are the subject of prayer and lays fast hold of the promise concerning it, as though it were for himself. He remains in the presence of God till God, by His Spirit, awakens the faith that in this matter the prayer has been heard.

In this way parents sometimes pray for their children, ministers for their congregations, laborers in God's vineyard for the souls committed to them, till they know that their prayer is heard. It is *the blood* that by its power of bringing us near to God bestows such wonderful liberty to pray until the answer is obtained.

Oh, if we understood more perfectly what it really means to dwell in the presence of God we surely would manifest more power in the exercise of our holy priesthood!

(2) *Instrumentally.*

A further manifestation of our priestly mediation is that we not only obtain some blessing for others by *intercession*, but we become the *instruments* by whom it is ministered. Every believer is called and should feel himself compelled by love to labor on behalf of others. He knows that God has blessed him that he might be a blessing to others; and yet the complaint is common that believers have no power for this work of bringing blessing to others. They are not, they say, in a condition to exercise an influence over others by their words. This is not to be wondered at if they will not dwell in the sanctuary. We read that "The Lord separated the tribe of Levi . . . to stand before the Lord . . . and to bless in His name" (Deuteronomy 10:8).

The priestly *power* of blessing depends on the priest-like *life* in the presence of God. He who experiences there the power of the blood to preserve him, the helpless one, will have courage to believe that the blood can certainly deliver others. For the holy,

life-giving power of the blood will create in him the same disposition as that in which Jesus shed it—the sacrifice of himself to
redeem others.

In faithful communion with God, our love will be set on fire
by the love of God; our belief that God will surely make use of us
will be strengthened; the Spirit of Jesus will take possession of us
to enable us to labor in humility, in wisdom and in power; and
our weakness and poverty will become the vessels in which God's
power can work. From our word and example *blessing* will flow
because we dwell with Him who is pure blessing . . . and He will
not permit anyone to be near Him without being also filled with
His blessing.

Beloved, is not the life prepared for us a glorious and a blessed
one? There is enjoyment of the blessedness of being near to God,
the carrying out of the ministry of His house, the imparting of
His blessing to others.

Let no one think that the full blessing is not for him, that
such a life is too high for him. *In the power of Jesus' blood* we have
the assurance that this "drawing near" is for us also, if only we
wholly yield ourselves to it.

For those who truly desire this blessing I give the following
advice:

(1) Remember that this, and nothing less, is designed for
you. All of us who are God's children have been brought near by
the blood. All of us can desire the full experience of it. Let us
only hold this fast: the life in *communion with God* is for *me*. The
Father does not wish that one of His children should be afar off.
In fact, we cannot please our God as we ought if we live without
this blessing. We are priests! Grace to live as priests is prepared
for us; free entrance into the sanctuary as our abiding place is
also for us. We can be assured of this! God bestows on us His

holy presence for indwelling as our *right*, for we are His children. Let us lay firm hold of this.

(2) Seek to make the full power of Jesus' blood *your own possession* in *all* its blessed effects. It is in the power of the blood that this glorious *communion with God* is possible. Let your heart be filled with faith in the power of the blood for *reconciliation*. Sin has been so entirely atoned for, and blotted out, that its power to keep you away from God has been completely and forever taken away! *Live* in the joyful declaration that sin is powerless to separate you one moment from God! *Believe* that by the blood you have been fully justified and thus have a righteous claim to a place in the sanctuary! Let the blood continually *cleanse* you. *Expect*, as an outgrowth from the fellowship that follows, an inner deliverance from the defilement of sin which still dwells in you! Say with the Scriptures: "How much more shall the blood of Christ cleanse *my* conscience to serve the living God." Let the blood *sanctify* you—separate you for God, in undivided consecration, to be filled by Him. Let the *pardoning, cleansing, sanctifying* power of the blood have free course in you. You will discover how this brings you automatically near to God and protects you.

(3) Do not fear to expect that *Jesus Himself* will reveal in you the power of the blood to bring you near to God.

The blood was shed to unite us to God.

The blood has accomplished its work and will perfect it in you.

The blood has unspeakable virtue and glory in God's sight.

The mercy seat sprinkled with blood is the chosen place of God's abode and is His throne of grace. He draws near with joy and good pleasure to the heart that surrenders itself entirely to the efficacy of the blood.

The blood has irresistible power. Through the blood Jesus was raised up from the grave and carried into heaven. Be assured the blood is able to preserve you every day in God's presence by its divine life-giving power.

As precious and all-powerful as the blood is, so sure and certain is also your abiding with God if only your trust is steadfast.

"Washed and made white in the blood of the Lamb—therefore they are before the throne of God and serve Him day and night in His temple." That word about the eternal glory has a bearing also upon our life on earth. The fuller one's faith and one's experience of the power of the blood, the closer the communion with God and the more sure the abiding near the throne. Likewise the wider will be one's entrance into the unbroken ministry of God in His sanctuary. And as regards our vocation here on earth now—the greater will be the power to serve the living God and the richer the priestly blessing you will spread around you. O Lord, may this word have its full power over us now, here and hereafter!

7

Dwelling in "the Holiest"
Through the Blood

"Therefore, brethren, having boldness to enter into the Holiest by the blood of Jesus, by a new and living way which He consecrated for us, through the veil, that is, His flesh, and having a High Priest over the house of God, let us draw near with a true heart in full assurance of faith, having our hearts sprinkled from an evil conscience and our bodies washed with pure water"—Hebrews 10:19–22.

IN THESE words we have a summary of the chief contents of this Epistle and the "good news" about God's grace as the Holy Spirit thus caused it to be presented to the Hebrews, and also to us.

Through sin man was driven out of Paradise, away from the presence and fellowship of God. God in His mercy sought from the beginning to restore the broken fellowship.

To this end He gave to Israel, through the shadowy types of the tabernacle, the expectation of a time to come when the wall of partition would be removed so that His people might dwell in His presence. "When shall I come and appear before God?" was the longing sigh of the saints of the Old Covenant.

It is the sigh also of many of God's children under the New Covenant who do not understand that the way into "the Holiest" has really been opened and that every child of God may and ought to have his real dwelling place there.

Oh, my brothers and sisters who long to experience the full power of the redemption which Jesus has accomplished, come with me to hear what our God says to us about the opened Holy of Holies and the freedom with which we can enter through the blood.

The passage at the beginning of this chapter shows us in a first series of four words *what* God has prepared for us as the sure ground on which our fellowship with Him may rest. Then in a second series of four words which follow, we learn *how* we may be prepared to enter into that fellowship and to live in it.

Read the text with attention and you will see that the words "Let us draw near" are the center of it all. This outline may be helpful:

    I. What God has prepared for us:
1. "The Holiest"—that is, the Most Holy Place.
2. The blood of Jesus.
3. A new and living way.
4. A High Priest.

    II. How God prepares us for what He has prepared for us:
1. A true heart.
2. Full assurance of faith.
3. Hearts sprinkled from an evil conscience.
4. Bodies washed with pure water.

Read the text now with an eye on this outline. "Therefore, brethren, having boldness to enter into *the Holiest*, by *the blood of Jesus*, by *a new and living way*, which He consecrated for us, through the veil, that is, His flesh, and having *a High Priest* over the house of God . . .

LET US DRAW NEAR

with *a true heart*, in *full assurance of faith*, having *our hearts cleansed from an evil conscience*, and *our bodies washed with pure water*."

I. What God Has Prepared for Us.

(1) "*The Holiest.*"

"Therefore having boldness to enter into the Holiest . . . , let us draw near."

To bring us into "the Holiest" is the goal of the redemptive work of Jesus, and he who does not know what "the Holiest" is cannot enjoy the full benefit of redemption.

What is this "Holiest"? It is just the place where God dwells. This does not refer only to heaven but to the *spiritual* Most Holy Place of God's presence.

Under the Old Covenant there was a material sanctuary (Hebrews 9:1 and 8:2)—the dwelling place of God, in which the priest dwelt in God's presence and served Him. Under the New Covenant there is the true *spiritual* tabernacle, not confined to any place. "The Holiest" is where God reveals Himself (John 4:23–26).

What a glorious privilege it is to enter into "the Holiest" and dwell there—to walk all day in the presence of God. What a rich blessing is poured out there. In "the Holiest" the favor and fellowship of God are enjoyed, the life and blessing of God are experienced, the power and joy of God are found. Life is spent in "the Holiest" in priestly purity and consecration and there incense with a sweet savor is burned and sacrifices acceptable to God are offered. It is a holy life of prayer and blessedness.

Under the Old Covenant everything was material, and the sanctuary also was material and local. Under the New Covenant everything is spiritual, and the true sanctuary owes its existence to the power of the Holy Spirit. Through the Holy Spirit a real life in "the Holiest" is possible and the knowledge that God walks there can be as certain as in the case of the priests of old. The Spirit makes real in our experience the work Jesus has accomplished.

Believer in Jesus Christ, have you liberty to enter into and abide in "the Holiest"? As one who has been redeemed, it is a fitting thing for you to make your home there and not elsewhere, for Christ cannot elsewhere reveal the full power of His redemption. But there, yes, *there* He can bless you richly. Do understand this then, and let the object of God and of our Lord Jesus be yours also. May it be the one desire of our hearts to enter into "the Holiest," to live in "the Holiest," to minister in "the Holiest." We can confidently expect the Holy Spirit to give us a right conception of the glory of entering into a dwelling in "the Holiest."

(2) *Liberty through the blood.*

Admission to "the Holiest," like "the Holiest" itself, belongs to God. God Himself thought of it and prepared it—and we have the liberty, the freedom, the right, to enter by the blood of Jesus. The blood of Jesus exercises such a wonderful power that through it a redeemed son of perdition may obtain full freedom to enter into the divine sanctuary, the Holy of Holies. "You who once were far off have been made near by the blood of Christ" (Ephesians 2:13).

And how does the blood exercise this wonderful power?

Scripture says "the life is in the blood" (Leviticus 17:11). The power of the blood is in the worth of the life. In the blood of Jesus the power of the divine life dwelt and worked. So the blood in His veins already possessed almighty and unceasing power. But that power could not be exercised for *reconciliation* until His blood was *shed.* By bearing the punishment of sin—death—the Lord Jesus conquered the power of sin and brought it to naught.

"The strength of sin is the law" (1 Corinthians 15:56). By perfectly fulfilling the law when He shed His blood under its curse, His blood has made sin entirely powerless. So the blood has its wonderful power not only because the life of God's Son was in it, but because it was *given as atonement for sin.* This is the reason Scripture speaks so highly about the blood.

Through the blood of the everlasting covenant, God has brought up our Lord Jesus from the dead (Hebrews 13:20). The power of Jesus' blood entirely destroyed the power of sin, death, the grave and hell—so that He, our Surety, could depart. And the power of the blood has opened heaven—so that there our Surety could freely enter.

With His own blood Jesus entered into "the Holiest" (Hebrews 9:12). And now *we also* have liberty to enter through the blood. Sin had taken away our liberty of approach to God, but the blood perfectly restored to us this liberty. He who will take time to meditate upon the power of the blood, appropriating it believingly for himself, will obtain a wonderful view of the liberty and directness with which we can now have communion with God.

Oh, the divine, wonderful power of the blood! Through the blood we enter into "the Holiest." The blood pleads *for* us and *in* us with an eternal, ceaseless effect. It removes sin from God's sight and from our conscience. Every moment we have free, full entrance so that we may have vivifying communion with God through the blood.

Oh, that the Holy Spirit might reveal to us the full power of the blood! Under His teaching what unrestricted entrance we enjoy to intimate fellowship with the Father. Our life is in "the Holiest" *through the blood.*

(3) *A new and living way.*
"Therefore, brethren, having boldness to enter into the Holiest by the blood of Jesus, by a new and living way, which He consecrated for us through the veil, that is, His flesh."

Jesus' blood bestows our *right* of entrance. The *way*, being a living and life-giving one, bestows the *power.* He consecrated this way through His flesh—and this is not a repetition in other words of the same thought as "through His blood." By no means.

Jesus shed His blood for us—in that aspect we cannot follow Him. But the way in which He walked when He shed His blood—

the rending of the veil of His flesh—in that way we *must* follow Him. For what He accomplished in the opening of that way provides a living power which draws and carries us as *we* enter "the Holiest." The lesson we have to learn here is this: the way into "the Holiest" is through *the rent veil of the flesh.*

In the tabernacle, the Most Holy Place was separated from the Holy Place by a veil. This veil is a symbol of our flesh. Yes, the veil that separates God and us is the flesh. Sin has its power in the flesh, and only through Jesus' taking away of sin could this divider be removed. Because Jesus came in human flesh He could rend the veil only by dying, and in that way render ineffective the power of the flesh and sin. "He offered up the flesh, and delivered it to death." This is what gave to the shedding of His blood its worth and power.*

And this remains now the law for each one who desires to enter "the Holiest" through Jesus' blood: *it must be through the rent veil of the flesh.* The blood both requires *and accomplishes* the rending of the flesh. Where the blood of Jesus is working powerfully, there always follows the putting to death of the flesh. He who desires to spare his flesh cannot enter into "the Holiest." The flesh must be sacrificed, given over to death. To whatever degree the believer perceives the sinfulness of his flesh and puts to death all that is in the flesh, to that extent he will understand and experience the power of the blood. The believer does this not in his own strength, but he comes by "a living way" which Jesus has consecrated, for the life-giving power of Jesus works in this "way." Remember, the Christian is crucified and dead with Jesus: "They that are Christ's have crucified the flesh." So it is in fellowship with Christ that we enter through the veil.

How glorious is this way—"the new and living way," full of

---

* For a fuller exposition of this important topic, see *The Holiest of All*, the author's complete devotional exposition of the book of Hebrews (130 chapters); or see *Let Us Draw Nigh*, which in twelve short chapters deals specifically with Hebrews 10:19–25.

life-giving power, which Christ "has consecrated for us"! *By this way* we have liberty to enter into "the Holiest" by the blood of Jesus. May the Lord God lead us along this "way," through the rent veil, through the death of the flesh to the full life of the Spirit. Then we shall find our dwelling place behind the veil, in "the Holiest" with God. Each sacrifice of the flesh leads us, through the blood, further into "the Holiest."

(4) *The High Priest.*

"And having a High Priest over the house of God, let us draw near."

Praised be God, we have not only the *work* but the *living person* of Christ as we enter "the Holiest"! Not only the blood and the living way, but *Jesus Himself* as "High Priest over the house of God."

The priests who went into the earthly sanctuary could do so only because of their relationship to the high priest, and none but the sons of Aaron were priests. We have an entrance into "the Holiest" because of our relationship to the Lord Jesus. He said to the Father, "Here am I and the children whom You have given Me."

Jesus is the High Priest. The Epistle to the Hebrews has shown us that He is the true Melchizedek, the eternal Son, who has an eternal and changeless priesthood, and as Priest is seated on the throne. He lives there to pray always; therefore He is able "to save to the uttermost those who come to God through Him." A great and all-powerful Priest!

As *High Priest over the house of God*, He is appointed over the entire ministry of "the Holiest." All the people of God are under His care. If we desire to enter "the Holiest," He is there to *receive* us, and to *present us to the Father.* He Himself will complete in us the sprinkling of the blood. Through the blood *He* has entered; through the blood He brings *us* in also. He will teach us all the duties of "the Holiest" and about our fellowship with God there. He makes acceptable our prayers, our offerings, and the duties of our ministry, however weak they are. What is more, He bestows on us heavenly light and heavenly power for our work and life in "the Holiest." It is He who imparts the life and the Spirit of "the Holiest." Just as His blood procured an entrance, His sacrifice of His flesh is the living way. As we enter, it is *He* by whom we are kept abiding there so that we are able always to walk well pleasing to God. As the sympathetic High Priest He knows how to stoop to each one, even the weakest. Yes, that is what makes intimate fellowship with God in "the Holiest" so attractive: we find Jesus there, as a "High Priest over the house of God."

And just when it seems to us as if "the Holiest" is too high or too holy for us, and that we cannot understand what the power of the blood is and how we are to walk on "the new and living way," just then we may look up to the living Savior Himself to teach us and to bring us Himself into "the Holiest." He is the Priest over the house of God. You have only to cleave to Him and you will be in "the Holiest."

"*Let us draw near*," seeing we have "the Holiest" where God waits for us, and the blood which gives us liberty, and the living way which carries us, and the High Priest to help us. "*Let us draw near*"—yes, "*let us draw near*." Let nothing hold us back from making use of these wonderful blessings which God designed for us. It is into "the Holiest" that we are to enter; our right has been obtained for us by the blood of Jesus, and by His own footsteps He has consecrated the way. He lives in His eternal priesthood to receive us in "the Holiest," to sanctify, to preserve, to bless us. Oh, let us no longer hesitate or turn back. Let us sacrifice all for this one thing. In view of what God has prepared for us, "let us draw near," led by the hand of Jesus, to appear before our Father and to find our life in the light of His countenance.

And so we desire to know *How can we now be prepared to*

enter? Our text gives us a glorious answer to this question.

II. How We Are Prepared.

Let us draw near—

(1) *With a true heart.*

This is the first of the four demands made on the believer who wishes to draw near. It is coupled with the second demand, *"in full assurance of faith,"* and it is chiefly in its union with the second that we understand aright what "a true heart" means.

The preaching of the gospel begins always with repentance and faith. Man cannot receive God's grace by faith if at the same time sin is not forsaken. In the progress of the life of faith this law is always binding. The full assurance of faith cannot be reached without "a true heart"—a heart that is wholly honest with God, that is surrendered entirely to Him. "The Holiest" cannot be entered without "a true heart"—a heart that is truly desirous in seeking what it professes to seek.

"Let us draw near with a true heart"—a heart that truly desires to forsake everything to dwell in "the Holiest," to possess God. A heart that truly abandons everything in order to yield itself to the authority and power of the blood. A heart that truly chooses the "new and living way" in order to go through the veil with Christ by the rending of the flesh. A heart that truly and entirely gives itself to the indwelling and lordship of Jesus.

"Let us draw near with a true heart." Without a true heart there is no entrance into "the Holiest."

But who has a true heart? *The new heart that God has given is a true heart.* Recognize that. By the power of the Spirit of God who dwells in that new heart, place yourself, by an exercise of your will, on the side of God against the sin that is still in your flesh. Say to the Lord Jesus, the High Priest, that you submit and cast down before Him every sin and all of your self-life, forsaking all to follow Him.

And as regards the hidden depths of sin in your flesh of which you are not yet conscious, and the malice of your heart—for them also provision is made. "Search me, O God, and know my heart." Subject yourself continually to the heart-searching light of the Spirit. He will uncover what is hidden from you. He who does this has a true heart to enter into "the Holiest."

(2) *In full assurance of faith.*

We know what place faith occupies in God's dealings with man. "Without faith it is impossible to please Him." Here at the entrance into "the Holiest" all depends on the "full assurance of faith."

There must be a "full assurance of faith" that there is a Most Holy Place where we can dwell and walk with God and that the power of the precious blood has conquered sin so perfectly that nothing can prevent our undisturbed fellowship with God. And full assurance that the way which Jesus has sanctified through His flesh is *a living way* which with eternal, living power carries those who tread on it. And full assurance that the High Priest over the house of God can save to the uttermost those who come to God through Him—that by His Spirit He works in us everything that is necessary for life in "the Holiest." These things we must believe and hold fast in "full assurance of faith."

But how can I get there? How can my faith grow to this full assurance? By fellowship with "Jesus who is the perfecter of faith" (Hebrews 12:2). As the High Priest over the house of God, He enables us to appropriate faith. By considering Him, His wonderful love, His perfect work, His precious and all-powerful blood, our faith is sustained and strengthened. God has given Him to awaken faith. By keeping our eyes fixed on Him, faith and the full assurance of faith become ours.

In handling the Word of God remember that "faith comes by

hearing, and hearing by the word of God." Faith *comes* by the Word and *grows* by the Word, but not the Word as *letter* but as the *voice of Jesus.* Only "the words that *I speak unto you*" are Spirit-life, only in *Him* are the promises of God "Yea and Amen." Take time to meditate on the Word and treasure it in your heart, but always with a heart set *on Jesus Himself.* It is faith *in Jesus* that saves. The Word that is taken to Jesus in prayer, and talked over with *Him*, is the Word that is effective.

Remember that "to him who has shall be given." Make use of the faith that you have; exercise it, declare it, and let your believing trust in God become the chief occupation of your life. God wishes to have children who believe Him; He desires nothing so much as faith. Get accustomed to say with each prayer, "Lord, I believe that I shall obtain this." As you read each promise in Scripture say, "Lord, I believe You will fulfill this in me." The whole day through, make it your holy habit in everything—yes, in everything—to exercise trust in God's guidance and God's blessing.

To enter into "the Holiest" "full assurance of faith" is necessary. "Let us draw near in full assurance of faith." Redemption through the blood is so perfect and powerful, the love and grace of Jesus so overflowing, the blessedness of dwelling in "the Holiest" is *so surely for us and within our reach*—"Let us draw near in full assurance of faith."

(3) *The heart sprinkled.*

Let us draw near ". . . having our hearts sprinkled from an evil conscience."

The heart is the center of human life, and the conscience again is the center of the heart. By his conscience man realizes his relationship to God, and an evil conscience tells him that all is not right between God and himself—not merely that he commits sin, but that he is *sinful* and *alienated* from God. A good or clear conscience bears witness that he is well pleasing to God (Hebrews 11:5). It bears witness not only that his sins are forgiven but that his heart is sincere before God. He who desires to enter "the Holiest" must have his heart *cleansed from an evil conscience.* The words are translated "our hearts sprinkled from an evil conscience." The blood of Christ will purify your conscience to serve the living God.

We have already seen that entrance to "the Holiest" is by the blood, by which Jesus went in to the Father. But that is not enough. There is a twofold sprinkling—the priests who drew near to God were not only *reconciled through the sprinkling of blood before God on the altar but their very persons must be sprinkled with the blood.* The blood of Jesus must be so brought by the Holy Spirit into direct contact with our hearts that our hearts become cleansed from an evil conscience. The blood removes all self-condemnation. It cleanses the conscience. Conscience then witnesses that the removal of guilt has been so perfectly completed that there is no longer the least separation between God and us. Conscience bears witness that we are well pleasing to God, that our heart is cleansed, that we through the sprinkling of the blood are in true, living fellowship with God. Yes, the blood of Jesus Christ cleanses from all sin, not only from the *guilt* but also from the *stain* of sin.

Through the power of the blood our fallen nature is prevented from exercising *its* power. Just as a fountain by its gentle spray cleanses the grass that otherwise would be covered with dust and keeps it fresh and green, so the blood works with a ceaseless effect to keep the soul clean. A heart that lives under the full power of the blood is a clean heart, cleansed from a guilty conscience, prepared to "draw near" with perfect freedom. The whole heart, the whole inner being is cleansed by a divine operation.

"Let us draw near . . . , having our hearts sprinkled from an evil conscience." Let us "in full assurance of faith" believe that our hearts are cleansed. Let us honor the blood greatly by confessing before God that it cleanses us. The High Priest will, by His Holy Spirit, make us understand the full meaning and power of the words: "having the heart cleansed by the blood." Entrance to the Most Holy Place is prepared through the blood; and further, our hearts are prepared by the blood for entrance. Oh, how glorious then, having the heart cleansed, to enter into and to abide in "the Holiest"!

(4) *The body washed.*
Let us draw near . . . "having . . . our bodies washed with pure water."

We belong to two worlds, the seen and the unseen. We have an inner, hidden life that brings us into touch with God, and an outer, bodily life by which we are in relationship with man. If this word refers to the body, it refers to our entire life in the body with all its activities.

The heart must be sprinkled with blood, the body must be washed with clear water. When the priests were consecrated they were washed with water as well as sprinkled with blood (Exodus 29:4, 20–21). And if the high priest went into the Most Holy Place, there was not only the altar with its blood but also the laver with its water (Leviticus 16:2–5). So also Christ came by water and blood (1 John 5:6). He had His baptism with water and later with blood (Matthew 3:13–15, Luke 12:50).

There is for us *also* a twofold cleansing: with water and blood. Baptism with water is unto repentance for laying aside of sin: "Be baptized and wash away your sins." While the blood cleanses the heart—the inner man—baptism is the yielding of the body with all its visible life to separation from sin.

So, "let us draw near . . . , having our hearts sprinkled from an evil conscience and our bodies washed with pure water." The power of the blood to cleanse inwardly cannot be experienced unless we also *cleanse ourselves* from all filthiness of the flesh. The *divine* work of cleansing by the sprinkling of blood, the *human* work of cleansing by laying aside sin, are inseparable.

We must be clean to enter into "the Holiest." Just as you would never dream of entering into the presence of a king unwashed, so you cannot imagine that you could come into the presence of God in the Most Holy Place if you are not cleansed from every sin. In the blood of Christ that cleanses from all sin, God has bestowed on you the power to cleanse yourself. Your desire to live with God in "the Holiest" must always be united with the most careful laying aside of even the least sin. The unclean may not enter "the Holiest."

Praise God, He desires to have us there. As His priests we must minister to Him there. He desires our purity that we may enjoy the blessing of "the Holiest," that is, His holy fellowship, and He has taken care that through the blood and by the Spirit we may be clean.

Let us each draw near, having our heart cleansed and our body washed with pure water.

"LET US DRAW NEAR."

The Holiest Place is accessible even to those among us who have not yet truly turned to the Lord. For them also the sanctuary has been opened. The precious blood, the living way and the High Priest are for them also. With great confidence we dare to invite even them: "Let us draw near." Despise not, my friends still far from God, oh, despise no longer God's wonderful grace. Draw near to the Father who has so earnestly sent this invitation to you. At the cost of the blood of His Son, God has opened a way for you into "the Holiest" and He waits in love to receive you into His dwelling place as His child. Oh, I beseech you, let us all draw near. Jesus Christ, the High Priest over the house of

God, is a perfect Savior.

"LET US DRAW NEAR."

"Let us draw near." The invitation comes especially to all believers. Don't be satisfied to stand in the courtyard of the tabernacle. It is not sufficient to cherish the hope that your sins are forgiven. "Let us draw near," let us enter behind the veil, let us in spirit press on to real nearness to our God. "Let us draw near" and live nearer to God and wholly take our abode in His holy presence. "Let us draw near" our place in the innermost sanctuary.

"Let us draw near with a true heart in full assurance of faith." He who gives himself sincerely and entirely to God will, through the Holy Spirit, experience "the full assurance of faith" to take for himself, freely and gladly, all that the Word has promised. Our weakness of faith arises from duplicity of heart. "Let us draw near with a true heart in full assurance" that the blessing is ours. The blood has so perfectly atoned for and conquered sin that nothing can hold the believer back from free admission to God.

"Let us draw near . . . , having our hearts sprinkled from an evil conscience and our bodies washed with pure water." Let us receive into our hearts *faith in the perfect power of the blood* and let us lay aside everything that is not in accord with the purity of the Most Holy Place. Then we shall begin to feel ourselves daily more at home in "the Holiest." In Christ, who is our Life, we are also there. Then we learn to carry on all our work in "the Holiest." All that we do is a spiritual sacrifice well pleasing to God in Jesus Christ. Brethren, "let us draw near" as God waits for us in "the Holiest."

"LET US DRAW NEAR."

That call has special reference to *prayer.* Not as though we, as priests, were not always in "the Holiest," but there are moments of more immediate fellowship when the soul turns itself entirely to God to be engaged with Him alone. Alas, our prayer is too often a calling out to God from a distance, so there is little power in it. Let us with each prayer first see that we are really in "the Holiest." Let us, with hearts perfectly sprinkled from an evil conscience, in silent faith appropriate the full effect of the blood by which sin as a separation between God and us is entirely removed. Yes, let us take time till we know that *right now* "I am in 'the Holiest' through the blood"—and *then* pray. That way we can lay our desires and wishes before our Father with assurance that they are an acceptable incense. Then prayer will truly be a "drawing near" to God, an exercise of inner fellowship with Him. Then we will have courage and power to carry on our work of priestly intercession and to pray down blessings on others. He who dwells in the Most Holy Place *through the power of the blood* is truly one of God's saints, and the power of God's holy and blessed presence goes out from him upon those who are round about him.

Brethren, "let us draw near": let us pray for ourselves, for one another, for everyone. Let "the Holiest" so become our fixed abode that we may carry about with us everywhere the presence of our God. Let this be the fountain of life for us that grows from strength to strength, from glory to glory, always in "the Holiest" by the blood. Amen.

8

Life in the Blood

"Then Jesus said to them, 'Most assuredly, I say to you, unless you eat the flesh of the Son of Man and drink His blood, you have no life in you. Whoever eats My flesh and drinks My blood has eternal life, and I will raise him up at the last day. For My flesh is food indeed, and My blood is drink indeed. He who eats My flesh and drinks My blood abides in Me, and I in him'"—John 6:53–56.

"The cup of blessing which we bless, is it not the communion of the blood of Christ?"—1 Corinthians 10:16.

THE DRINKING of the blood of the Lord Jesus is the subject brought before us in these words. Just as water has a twofold effect, so is it also with this holy blood.

When water is used for washing it cleanses, but if we drink it we are refreshed and revived. He who desires to know the full power of the blood of Jesus must be taught by Him what the blessing of "drinking" the blood is. Everyone knows the difference there is between washing and drinking. Necessary and pleasant as it is to use water for cleansing, it is much more necessary and reviving to drink it. Without its cleansing it is not possible to live as we ought; but without drinking we cannot live at all. It is only by drinking that we enjoy the full benefit of its power to sustain life.

Without drinking the blood of the Son of God—that is, without the most hearty appropriation of it—eternal life cannot be obtained.

To many there seems to be something unpleasant in the phrase "drinking the blood of the Son of Man," but it was still more disagreeable to the Jews, for the use of blood was forbidden by the Law of Moses under severe penalties. When Jesus spoke of "drinking His blood" it not only naturally annoyed them, it was an *unspeakable offence* to their religious feelings. Our Lord, we may be sure, would not have used the phrase had He been able otherwise to make plain to them and to us the deepest and most glorious truths concerning salvation by the blood.

In seeking to become partakers of the salvation here spoken of as "drinking the blood of our Lord," let us endeavor to understand:

    I. What the blessing is which is described as "drinking the blood."

   II. How this blessing is worked out in us.

  III. What should be our attitude toward it.

I. What the Blessing Is Which Is Described as "Drinking the Blood."

We saw just now that drinking expresses a much more intimate connection with water than washing, and hence produces a more powerful effect. There is a blessing in one's fellowship with the blood of Jesus which goes much farther than either cleansing or sanctification. I trust that we shall see how far-reaching is the influence of the blessing indicated by this phrase.

Not only must the blood do something *for* us, by placing us in a new relationship to God, but it must do something *in* us, entirely renewing us within. It is to this that the words of the Lord Jesus draw our attention when He says: "Unless you eat the flesh of the Son of man and drink His blood, you have no life in you." Our Lord distinguishes two kinds of life. The Jews there in His presence had a natural life of body and soul. Many among them were devout, well-intentioned men, but He said they had no life in them unless they "ate His flesh and drank His blood." They needed another life, a new heavenly life, which He possessed and which only He could impart.

All creature life must obtain nourishment outside of itself. Natural life is naturally nourished, by bread and water. Heavenly life must be nourished by heavenly food and drink, by Jesus Himself. "Unless you eat the flesh of the Son of man and drink His blood, you have no life in you." Nothing less must become ours than His life—the life that He, as Son of man, lived on earth.

Our Lord emphasized this still more strongly in the words which follow, in which He again explained what the nature of that life is: "Whoever eats My flesh and drinks My blood has eternal life, and I will raise him up at the last day." Eternal life is the life of God. Our Lord came to earth, in the first place, to *reveal* this eternal life—reveal it *in the flesh*—and then to *communicate* it to *us* who are in the flesh. In Him we see the eternal life dwelling in its divine power in a body of flesh which was later taken up into heaven. He tells us that those who eat His flesh and drink His blood, who partake of His body as their sustenance, will experience also in their own bodies the power of eternal life. "I will raise him up at the last day." The marvel of the eternal life in Christ is that it was eternal life *in a human body*. We must become partakers of that body as well as of the activities of His spirit; then our body, also possessing that life, will one day be raised from the dead.

Our Lord said: "My flesh is food indeed, and My blood is drink indeed." The word translated "indeed" here is the same as that He used when He spoke His parable of the True Vine, "I am the *true* [the 'indeed'] vine," thus indicating the difference between what was only a symbol and what is actual truth. Earthly food is no *real* food for it imparts no *real life*. The one *true* food is the body and blood of the Lord Jesus Christ *which imparts and sustains life*, and that in no shadowy or merely symbolical manner. No, this word so frequently repeated indicates that in a full and real sense the flesh and blood of the Lord Jesus are the food by which eternal life is nourished and sustained in us: "My flesh is food *indeed*, and My blood is drink *indeed*."

In order to point out the reality and power of this food, our Lord added: "He who eats My flesh and drinks My blood abides in Me, and I in him." Nourishment by His flesh and blood effects the most perfect union with Him. This is the reason that His flesh and blood have such power of eternal life. Our Lord declares here that those who believe in Him are to experience not only certain influences from Him in their hearts, but are to be brought into the most close and abiding union with Him. "He who drinks My blood abides in Me, and I in Him."

This, then, is the blessing of drinking the blood of the Son of man—becoming one with Him, becoming a partaker of the divine nature in Him. How real this union is may be seen from the words which follow: "As I live because of the Father, so he who feeds on Me will live because of Me." Nothing except the union which exists between our Lord and the Father can serve as a type of our union with Him. Just as in the indivisible divine nature the two Persons are truly one, so man becomes one in human nature with Jesus. The union is just as real as that in the divine nature, only with this difference, that as human nature cannot exist apart from the body, this union includes the body also.

Our Lord "prepared for Himself" a human body into which He engrafted a corporate body of believers. This body became, by the body and blood of Jesus, a sharer in eternal life, in the life of our Lord Himself. Those who desire to receive the fullness of this blessing must be careful to enjoy all that the Scripture offers them in the holy, mysterious expression "to drink the blood of Christ."

II. How This Blessing Is Worked Out in Us—or, What the "Drinking of the Blood of Jesus" Really Is.

The first idea that here presents itself is that "drinking" indicates the deep, true appropriation in our spirit, by faith, of all we understand concerning the power of the blood.

We speak sometimes of "drinking in" the words of a speaker, when we heartily give ourselves up to listen and receive them. So when the heart of anyone is filled with a sense of the preciousness and power of the blood . . . when he, with real joy, is lost in the contemplation of it . . . when he, with wholehearted faith, takes it for himself and seeks to be convinced in his inner being of the life-giving power of that blood, then it may be rightly said that he "drinks the blood of Jesus." All that faith enables him to see of *redemption*, of *cleansing*, of *sanctification* by the blood, he absorbs into the depths of his soul.

There is a deep truth in this representation and it gives us a very glorious demonstration of the way in which the full blessing by the blood may be obtained. And yet it is certain that our Lord intended something more than this by so repeatedly making use of the expression about "eating His flesh and drinking His blood." What this further truth is becomes clear by His institution of *the Lord's Supper.* For, although our Savior did not actually deal with that Supper when He taught in Capernaum, yet He spoke on the subject of which later on the Supper was made the visible confirmation.

In the Reformed Churches there are two aspects of viewing the Holy Supper. According to one which is called after the name of the Reformer Zwingli, the bread and wine in the Supper are merely tokens or representations of a spiritual truth, to teach us that *just as*, and *as sure as*, bread and wine when eaten or drunk nourish and revive, so surely—*and even more surely*—the body and blood recognized and appropriated by faith, nourish and quicken the soul.

According to the other view, which bears the name of Calvin, there is something more than this in the eating of the Supper. He teaches that in a hidden and incomprehensible way, but yet really, we, through the Holy Spirit, become so nourished *by the body and blood of Jesus in heaven* that even our body, through the power of His body, becomes a partaker in the power of eternal life. Hence he connects the resurrection of the body with the eating of Christ's body in the Supper. He writes thus: "The bodily presence which the Sacrament demands is such, and exercises such a power here [in the Supper] that it becomes not only the undoubted assurance in our spirit of eternal life but also assures the immortality of the flesh. If anyone asks me how this can be, I am not ashamed to acknowledge that it is a mystery too high for my spirit to comprehend, or my words to express. I feel it more than I can understand it.

"It may seem incredible indeed that the flesh of Christ should reach us from such an immense local distance so as to become our food. But we must remember how far the power of the Holy Spirit transcends all our senses. Let faith then embrace what the understanding cannot grasp, namely: The sacred communication of His flesh and blood by which Christ transfuses His life into us, just as if it penetrated our bones and marrow."

The communion of the flesh and blood of Christ is necessary for all who desire to inherit eternal life. The Apostle Paul says: "The church . . . is His body" (Ephesians 1:23). "He is the head from whom the whole body, joined and knit together . . . , causes growth of the body" (Ephesians 4:15–16). Our bodies are members of Christ (1 Corinthians 6:15–16). We see that all this cannot take place if He is not attached to us in body and spirit. The Apostle again makes use of a glorious expression, "We are members of His body, of His flesh and of His bones" (Ephesians 5:30). Then he cries out, "The mystery is great!" It would therefore be folly not to recognize the communion of believers in the body and blood of the Lord—a communion which the Apostle esteemed so great that he wondered at it, rather than explained it.

There is something more in the Supper than simply the believer appropriating the redemptive work of Christ. This is made clear in the Heidelberg Catechism in Question 76: "What does it mean to eat the crucified body of Christ and to drink His shed blood?" The answer is: "It is not only to embrace with a believing heart all the sufferings and death of Christ and thereby to receive pardon of sin and eternal life; but also, besides that, to become more and more united to His sacred body, by the Holy Spirit who dwells at once both in Christ and in us; so that we, though Christ is in heaven and we on earth, are, notwithstanding, flesh of His flesh and bone of His bones; and we live and are governed forever by one Spirit."

The thoughts that are expressed in this teaching are in entire agreement with Scripture.

In the creation of man the remarkable thing which distinguishes him from the spirits which God had previously created and which was to make man the crowning work of God's wisdom and power was that he would reveal the life of the spirit and the glory of God in a body formed out of dust. However, through the body lust and sin came into the world. Full redemption is designed to deliver the body and to make it God's abode. Redemption will be perfect and God's purpose accomplished only then. This was the purpose for which the Lord Jesus came in the flesh, and in Him dwelt "all the fullness of the Godhead bodily." For this He bore our sins in His body on the tree, and by His death and resurrection He delivered the body as well as the spirit from the power of sin and death. As the firstfruits of this redemption we are now one body as well as one spirit with Him. We are of His body, of His flesh and of His bones. Because of this, in the observance of the Holy Supper the Lord comes to the body *also* and takes possession of it. Not only does He work by

His Spirit on our *spirit* so as to make our body share in redemption at the resurrection. No, already, *here*, the body is the *temple* of the Spirit, and the sanctification of the soul and spirit will progress the more gloriously just in proportion as the undivided personality, including the body—which exercises such an opposing influence—has a share in it.

Thus we are in the Sacrament intentionally fed by "the real natural body and the real blood of Christ." Not following the teaching of Luther, that the body of Christ is so in the bread that even an *un*believer eats the holy body, but "real" in the sense that faith, in a secret way, by the Spirit, really receives *the power of the holy body and blood from heaven* as the food by which soul and body become partakers of eternal life.

All that has now been said about the Supper must have its full application to "the drinking of the blood of Jesus." It is a deep spiritual mystery in which the most intimate, the most perfect union with Christ, is effected. It takes place where the soul, through the Holy Spirit, fully appropriates the communion of the blood of Christ and becomes a true partaker of the very *attitude* which He revealed in the shedding of His blood. The blood is the soul, the life of the body; where the believer as one body with Christ desires to abide perfectly in Him, there, through the Spirit, in a superhuman, powerful way, the blood will support and *strengthen* the heavenly life. The life that was poured out in the blood becomes *his* life. The life of the old "I" dies to make room for the life of Christ in him. By perceiving how this drinking is the highest participation in the heavenly life of the Lord, faith has one of its highest and most glorious offices.

III. What Should Be Our Attitude Toward This Drinking?

Beloved brethren, you have already heard that we have here one of the deepest mysteries of the life of God in us. We should draw near with very deep reverence while we ask the Lord Jesus to teach us and bestow upon us what He means by this "drinking of His blood."

Only he who longs for full union with Jesus will learn correctly what it is to drink the blood of Jesus. "He who drinks My blood abides in Me, and I in him." He who is satisfied with just the forgiveness of his sins, he who does not thirst to be made to drink abundantly of the love of Jesus, he who does not desire to experience redemption for soul and body in its full power so as to have truly in himself the same disposition that was in Jesus, will have only a small share in "drinking of the blood." He who, on the other hand, sets before him as his chief object that which is also the object of Jesus: "abide in Me, and I in you"—who desires that the power of eternal life should operate in his body—he will not allow himself to be frightened by the impression that these words are too high or too mysterious. He longs to become heavenly minded because he belongs to heaven and is going there; therefore he desires to obtain his food and drink also from heaven. Without thirst there is no drinking. Longing after Jesus and for perfect fellowship with Him is the thirst which is the best preparation for drinking the blood.

It is by the Holy Spirit that the thirsty soul will be made ready to drink of the heavenly refreshment of this life-giving drink. We have already said that this drinking is a heavenly mystery. In heaven, where God the Judge of all is and where Jesus the Mediator of the New Covenant is, there also is "the blood of sprinkling" (Hebrews 12:23–24). When the Holy Spirit teaches us—taking us, as it were, by the hand—He bestows more than our merely human understanding can grasp. All the thoughts that we can entertain about the blood or the life of Jesus, about our share in that blood as members of His body, and about the impartation to us of the living power of the blood, all are but feeble rays of the glorious reality which He, the Holy Spirit, will bring into being in us through our union with Jesus.

Where in our human bodies do we find that our blood is actually received? Is it not natural that one member of the body after another, through the arteries, receives the bloodstream, which is continually renewed from the heart? Each member of a healthy body ceaselessly and abundantly "drinks in" the blood. In the same way, the Spirit of life in Christ Jesus, who unites us to Him, will make our drinking of Jesus' blood the natural action of the *inner* life. When the Jews complained that what the Lord had spoken concerning eating His flesh and drinking His blood was a "hard saying," He said, "It is the Spirit who gives life; the flesh profits nothing." It is the Holy Spirit who makes this divine mystery *life and power* in us, a true living experience in which we abide in Jesus and He in us.

There must be on our part a quiet, strong, settled expectancy of faith that this blessing will be bestowed on us. We must believe that all the precious blood can do is really for *us*.

Let us believe that the Savior Himself will cause us, through the Holy Spirit, to drink His blood unto life. Let us first of all believe and very heartily and continuously appropriate those effects of the blood which we understand better, namely its reconciling, cleansing, and sanctifying effects. We may then, with the greatest certainty and joy, say to the Lord: "O Lord, Your blood is my life drink! You who have washed and cleansed me by that blood, You will also teach me every day 'to eat the flesh of the Son of man and drink His blood' so that I may *abide* in You and You in me." He will surely do this.

9

Victory Through the Blood

"They overcame him by the blood of the Lamb and by the word of their testimony, and they did not love their lives to the death"—Revelation 12:11.

FOR THOUSANDS of years there had been a mighty conflict for the possession of mankind between the "old serpent," who led man astray, and "the Seed of the woman."

Often it seemed as though the kingdom of God had come in power; then at other times the might of evil obtained such supremacy that the strife appeared to be hopeless.

It was thus also in the life of our Lord Jesus. By His coming and His wonderful words and works, the most glorious expectations of a speedy redemption were awakened. How terrible was the disappointment which the death of Jesus brought to all who had believed in Him! It seemed, indeed, as if the powers of darkness had conquered and had established their kingdom forever.

But, behold! Jesus is risen from the dead! An apparent victory proved to be the terrible downfall of the prince of darkness. By bringing about the death of "the Lord of life" Satan permitted Him who alone was able to break open the gates of death to enter his kingdom. "Through death He has destroyed him who had the power of death, that is, the devil." In that holy moment when our Lord shed His blood in death and it seemed as if Satan were victorious, the adversary was robbed of the authority he had hitherto possessed.

Our text gives a very grand representation of these memorable events. The best commentators, notwithstanding differences in details of exposition, are united in thinking that we have here a vision of the casting out of Satan from heaven as a result of the ascension of Christ.

We read in verses 5 through 9: The woman "bore a male Child who . . . was caught up to God and to His throne. . . . And war broke out in heaven: Michael and his angels fought against the dragon; and the dragon and his angels fought, but they did not prevail, nor was a place found for them in heaven any longer. So, the great dragon was cast out, that serpent of old, called the Devil and Satan, who deceives the whole world; he was cast to the earth, and his angels were cast out with him."

Then follows the song from which the text is taken: "Now salvation, and strength, and the kingdom of our God, and the power of His Christ have come, for the accuser of our brethren, who accused them before our God day and night, has been cast down. And they overcame him by the *blood of the Lamb* and by the word of their testimony, and they did not love their lives to the death. Therefore rejoice, O heavens, and you who dwell in them!"

The point which deserves our special attention is that while the conquest of Satan and his being cast out of heaven is first represented as the result of the ascension of Jesus and the war in heaven which followed, yet in the song of triumph which was heard in heaven, victory is ascribed chiefly to *the blood of the Lamb*; this was the power by which the victory was gained.

Through the whole Book of Revelation we see the Lamb on the throne. It is as the slain Lamb that He has gained that position; *the victory over Satan and all his authority is by the blood of the Lamb.*

We have spoken about the blood in its manifold effects. It is fitting that we should seek to understand how it is that victory is always ascribed to *the blood of the Lamb*.

We shall consider victory:

    I. As gained once for all.

   II. As being progressive.

  III. As one in which we have a share.

I. The Victory Which Was Gained Once for All.

In the exalted representation given in our text we see what a high position was once occupied by Satan, the enemy of the human race. He had entrance into heaven and appeared there as the accuser of the brethren and as the opponent of whatever was done in the interests of God's people.

We know how this is taught in the Old Testament. In the Book of Job we see Satan coming with the angelic sons of God to present himself before the Lord and to obtain permission from Him to tempt His servant Job (Job 1). In the Book of Zechariah (3:1–2) we read that the prophet saw "Joshua the high priest standing before the Angel of the Lord, and Satan standing at his right hand to oppose him." Then there is also the statement of our Lord, recorded in Luke 10:18, "I saw Satan fall like lightning from heaven." Later on, in His agony of soul as He felt beforehand His approaching sufferings, Jesus said, "Now is the judgment of this world; now the ruler of this world will be cast out" (John 12:31).

It may, at first thought, seem strange that the Scriptures should represent Satan as being in heaven. To understand this correctly it is necessary to remember that heaven is not a small, circumscribed dwelling place where God and Satan had friendly communication as neighbors. No, heaven is an illimitable sphere with very many different divisions, filled with innumerable hosts of angels who carry out God's will in nature. Among them, Satan also still held a place. And remember, he is not represented in Scripture to be the black, grisly figure in outward appearance as he is generally pictured, but as "an angel of light." He was a prince with ten thousands of servants.

When he had brought about the fall of man and thus transferred the world to himself and became its prince, he had real authority over all that was in it. Man had been destined to be king of this world, for God had said, "Have dominion. . . ." When Satan conquered the king he took his entire kingdom under *his own* authority—and *this authority was recognized* by God. God, in His holy will, had ordained that if man listened to Satan, he must suffer the consequences and become subject to his tyranny. God never in this matter used His power or exercised force but always took the way of law and right, and so Satan retained his authority until it was taken from him in a lawful manner.

This is the reason why he could appear before God in heaven as accuser of the brethren and in opposition to them for the 4,000 years of the Old Covenant.

Satan had obtained authority over all flesh and only after he was conquered *in flesh, as the sphere of his authority*, could he be cast out forever, as accuser, from the Court of Heaven.

So the Son of God therefore had to come *in flesh*, in order to fight and conquer Satan *on his own ground.*

For this reason also, at the commencement of His public life, our Lord after His anointing—being thus openly recognized as the Son of God—"was led up by the Spirit into the wilderness to be tempted by the devil." Victory over Satan could be gained only after He had personally endured and resisted his temptations.

But even this victory was not sufficient. Christ came in order that "through death He might destroy him who had the power of death, that is, the devil." The devil had that power of death *because of the law of God*. That law has installed him as jailer of its prisoners. Scripture says: "The sting of death is sin, and the *strength of sin is the law*." Victory over and the casting out of Satan could not take place till the righteous demands of the law were perfectly fulfilled. The sinner must be delivered from the power of the law before he could be delivered from the authority of Satan.

It was through His death and the shedding of His blood that the Lord Jesus fulfilled the law's demands. Ceaselessly, the law had been declaring that "The wages of sin is death"; "The soul who sins shall die." By the typical ministry of the temple, by the sacrifices with the blood-shedding and blood-sprinking, the ceremonial law had foretold that redemption and reconciliation could take place only by the shedding of blood. As our Surety, the Son of God was born under the law. He obeyed it perfectly. He resisted the temptations of Satan to withdraw Himself from under its authority. He willingly gave Himself up to bear the punishment of sin. He gave no ear to the temptations of Satan to refuse the cup of suffering. When He shed His blood He had devoted His whole life, to its very end, to the fulfilling of the law. When the law had been thus perfectly fulfilled, the authority of sin and Satan was brought to an end. Therefore death could not hold Him. "Through the blood of the everlasting covenant" God brought Him "up from the dead." So also He "entered heaven with His own blood" to make His atonement effective for us.

The text gives us a striking description of the glorious result of the appearing of our Lord in heaven. We read concerning the mystic woman: "She bore a male Child who was to rule all nations with a rod of iron. And her Child was caught up to God and to His throne. . . . And war broke out in heaven: Michael and his angels fought against the dragon; and the dragon and his angels fought, but they did not prevail, nor was a place found for them in heaven any longer. So the great dragon was cast out, that serpent of old, called the Devil and Satan, who deceives the whole world; he was cast to the earth, and his angels were cast out with him." Then follows the song of victory in which the words of our text occur: "They overcame him by the *blood of the Lamb*."

In the Book of Daniel we read of a previous conflict between this Michael, who stood on the side of God's people Israel, and the opposing world powers. His strength was great. But only now can Satan be cast out—because of the blood of the Lamb. Atonement for sin and the fulfillment of the law have taken from Satan all his authority and right. The blood, as we have already seen, that had done such wonderful things in heaven with God, in blotting out sin and bringing it to naught, had a similar power over Satan. He has now no longer any right to accuse. "Now salvation, and strength, and the kingdom of our God, and the power of His Christ have come, for the accuser of our brethren . . . has been cast down. And they overcame him by the blood of the Lamb."

II. There Is a Progressive Victory, Which Follows After This First Victory. Satan Having Been Cast Down to Earth, the Heavenly Victory Must Now Be Carried Out Here.

This is indicated in the words of the song of victory, "They overcame him by the blood of the Lamb." This was primarily spoken concerning "the brethren" mentioned, but it refers also to the victory of the angels. Victory in heaven and on earth progress simultaneously, resting on the same ground. We know from the portion in Daniel already mentioned (Daniel 10:12–13) what fellowship there exists between heaven and earth in carrying on the work of God. As soon as Daniel prayed the angel became active, and the three weeks of strife in the heavenlies coincided with three weeks of prayer and fasting on earth. Conflict here on earth is the result of a conflict in the invisible region of the heavenlies. Michael and his angels, as well as the brethren on earth, gained the victory "by the blood of the Lamb."

In the twelfth chapter of Revelation we are clearly taught how the conflict was removed from heaven to earth. "Woe to the inhabitants of the earth!" exclaimed the voice in heaven. "For the devil has come down to you, having great wrath, because he knows that he has a short time." Then we read: "Now when the dragon saw that he had been cast to the earth, he persecuted the woman who gave birth to the male Child."

The woman signifies the people out of which Jesus was born. When the devil could not harm *Him* anymore, he persecutes those who are *His people.* The disciples of our Lord and the church in the first three centuries had experience of this. In the bloody persecutions in which hundreds of thousands of Christians perished as martyrs, Satan did his utmost to lead the church into apostasy or to root it out altogether. So in its full sense, the statement that "they overcame him by the blood of the Lamb and by the word of their testimony, and they did not love their lives to the death" applies to the martyrs.

After the centuries of persecution there came to the church centuries of rest and worldly prosperity. Satan had tried force in vain. By the favor of the world he might have better success. As the church conformed to the world everything became darker and darker, till in the Middle Ages the Romish apostasy reached its climax. Nevertheless, during all these ages there were many who in the midst of surrounding misery fought the fight of faith, and by the piety of their lives and witness for the Lord the statement was often established: "They overcame him by the blood of the Lamb and by the word of their testimony, and they did not love their lives to the death."

This was no less the secret power by which, through the blessed Reformation, the mighty authority which Satan had gained in the church was broken down. "They overcame him by the blood of the Lamb." It was the discovery and personal application and preaching of the glorious truth that we are "justified freely by His grace through the redemption that is in Christ Jesus, whom God set forth to be a propitiation by His blood, through faith," that gave to the Reformers such wonderful power and such a glorious victory.

Since the days of the Reformation it is still apparent that in proportion as the blood of the Lamb is gloried in, the church is constantly inspired by new life to obtain the victory over deadness and error. And to evangelize the world! Yes, in the midst of the wildest heathen, where the throne of Satan has been undisturbed for thousands of years, the blood is surely the weapon by which his power must be destroyed. The preaching of "the blood of the cross" as the propitiation for the sins of the world and the ground of God's free, forgiving love is the power by which even the most darkened heart is opened and softened, and is changed from being a dwelling place of Satan into a temple of the Most High.

What avails for the church is available also for each Christian. In "the blood of the Lamb" he always has victory. It is when a person is convinced of the power which that blood has with God in heaven—power to effect a perfect reconciliation through the blotting out of sin, power to rob the devil of his authority over us completely and forever, power to work out in our hearts a full assurance of the favor of God, power to destroy the might of sin—it is, I say, when a person lives in the power of the blood, that the temptations of Satan cease to ensnare.

Where the holy blood of the Lamb is sprinkled, there God dwells and Satan is put to flight. In heaven and on earth—and in our individual hearts—that word as the announcement of *a progressive victory* is valid: "They overcame him by the blood of the Lamb."

III. We Also Have a Share In This Victory—If We Are Reckoned Among Those Who Have Been Cleansed in the Blood of the Lamb.

To have the full enjoyment of this we must pay attention to the following facts:

(1) *There can be no victory without conflict.*

We must recognize that we dwell in an enemy's territory. What was revealed to the Apostle John in his heavenly vision must hold good in our daily lives. Satan has been cast down to the earth and has great wrath because he has only a short time. He cannot now reach the glorified Jesus but seeks to reach Him by attacking His people. We must live always under the holy consciousness that we are watched every moment by an enemy of unimaginable cunning and power who is unwearied in his endeavor to bring us entirely, or even partially—however little it may be—under his authority. He is literally "the ruler of this world." All that is in the world is ready to serve him, and he knows how to make use of it in his attempts to lead the church to be unfaithful to her Lord and to inspire her with *his* spirit—the spirit of the world.

He makes use not only of temptation to what is commonly recognized to be sin, but he knows how to obtain an entrance into our everyday activities. Into our seeking for daily bread and necessary money. Into our politics, our commercial ventures, our literature and science. Into our studies and times of relaxation. He knows how to make anything that is lawful in itself into a tool to forward his devilish deceptions.

The believer who desires to share in the victory over Satan "through the blood of the Lamb" must be a *fighter*. He must take pains to understand the character of his enemy. He must allow himself to be taught by the Spirit through the Word what the secret cunning of Satan is—what is called in Scripture "the depths of Satan," by which he so often blinds and deceives men. He must know that this strife is not against flesh and blood "but against spiritual hosts of wickedness in the heavenly places" (Ephesians 6:12). He must devote himself in every way and at all costs to carry on the conflict until death. Then only will he be able to join in the song of victory: "They overcame him by the blood of the Lamb and by the word of their testimony, and they did not love their lives to the death."

(2) *Victory is through faith.*

"*This is the victory that has overcome the world—our faith.* Who is he who overcomes the world but he who believes that Jesus is the Son of God?" (1 John 5:4–5). "Be of good cheer," said our Lord Jesus, "I have overcome the world." *Satan is an already-conquered enemy.* He has nothing, absolutely nothing *by right* to say against one who belongs to the Lord Jesus. By my unbelief, or by ignorance of or letting go my hold of the fact that I have a participation in the victory of Jesus, I may again give Satan authority over me which otherwise he does not possess. But when I know by a living faith that I am one with the Lord Jesus and that the Lord Himself lives in me, *maintaining and carrying on in me that victory which He gained*, then, Satan has no power over me. Victory through "the blood of the Lamb" is the strength of my life.

Only this faith can inspire courage and joy in the struggle. By thinking of the terrible power of the enemy, of his never-sleeping watchfulness, of the way in which he has taken possession of everything on earth by which to tempt us, it might well be said—as some Christians think—that the struggle is too severe, that it is not possible to live always under such tension. "Life would be impossible!" This is perfectly true if we in our weakness had to meet the enemy or gain the victory by our own might. But that is *not* what we are called upon to do. *Jesus is the Victor.* We need only have our souls filled with the heavenly vision of Satan being cast out of heaven by Jesus to maintain the power and victory of His blood. We need only be filled with faith in the blood by which Jesus Himself conquered, and with faith that He Himself is with us. Then we also are "more than conquerors through Him who loved us."

(3) *This victory of faith is in fellowship with the blood of the Lamb.*

Faith is not merely a thought of which I lay hold, a conviction that possesses me—*it is a life*! Faith brings the soul into direct contact with God and the unseen things of heaven, but above all, with the blood of Jesus. *It is not possible to believe in victory over Satan by the blood without being myself brought entirely under its power.*

Belief in the power of the blood awakens in me a desire for an experience of it as power in myself. And each experience of its power makes belief in victory more glorious.

Seek to enter more deeply into the *perfect reconciliation with God* which is yours. Live with assurance, constantly exercising faith in His promise that "the blood cleanses from all sin." Yield yourself to be sanctified and brought near to God through the blood: let it be your life-giving nourishment and power. You will thus have an unbroken experience of victory over Satan and his temptations. He who, as a consecrated priest, walks with God, will rule as a conquering king over Satan.

Believers, our Lord Jesus by His blood has made us not only priests but kings unto God, that we may draw near to God not only in priestly purity and ministry but that also in kingly power we may *rule for God.* A kingly spirit must inspire us—a kingly courage to rule over our enemies. The blood of the Lamb must increasingly be a token and seal not only of pardon from all guilt but of victory over all the power of sin!

The resurrection and ascension of Jesus and the casting out of Satan were the results of the shedding of His blood. And now in you the sprinkling of the blood will open the way for the full enjoyment of resurrection with Jesus, and of being seated with Him in the heavenly places.

Once more, therefore, I beseech you to open your entire being to the incoming of the power of the blood of Jesus. Then your life will become a continual observance of the resurrection and ascension of our Lord and a continual victory over all the powers of hell. Your heart, too, will constantly unite with the song of heaven: "Now salvation, and strength, and the kingdom of our God, and the power of His Christ have come, for the accuser of the brethren . . . has been cast down." Remember always, they overcame him by the blood of the Lamb.

10

Heavenly Joy Through the Blood

"After these things I looked, and behold, a great multitude which no one could number . . . standing before the throne and before the Lamb . . . and crying out with a loud voice, saying, 'Salvation belongs to our God who sits on the throne, and to the Lamb!' . . . 'Who are these arrayed in white robes?' . . . 'These are the ones who have come out of the great tribulation, and washed their robes and made them white in the blood of the Lamb'"—Revelation 7:9–14.

THESE WORDS occur in the well-known vision of the great multitude in heavenly glory which no one could number. In spirit the Apostle John saw them standing before the throne of God and of the Lamb, clothed in long, white robes and with palm branches in their hands, and singing with a loud voice, "Salvation belongs to our God who sits on the throne, and to the Lamb!" All the angels answered this song by falling down on their faces before the throne to worship God and to offer eternal praise and glory to Him.

Then one of the heavenly elders, pointing out the great multitude and the clothing which distinguished them, put the question to John, "Who are these arrayed in white robes, and where did they come from?" John replied, "Sir, you know." Then the elder said, "These are the ones who have come out of the great tribulation, and washed their robes and made them white in the blood of the Lamb. Therefore they are before the throne of God, and serve Him day and night in His temple."

This explanation, given by one of the elders who stood around the throne, concerning the state of the redeemed in their heavenly glory, is of great value. It reveals to us the fact that not only in this world of sin and strife is the blood of Jesus the one hope of the sinner, but that in heaven, when every enemy has been subdued, that precious blood will be recognized forever as the ground of our salvation. And we learn that the blood must exercise its power with God in heaven not only as long as sin has still to be dealt with here beneath, but that through all eternity each of the redeemed, to the praise and glory of the blood, will bear the sign of how the blood has availed for him and that he owes his salvation entirely to it.

If we have a clear insight into this we shall understand better what a true and vital connection there is between "the sprinkling of the blood" and the joys of heaven, and that a true intimate connection with the blood will enable the believer while still on earth to share the joy and glory of heaven.

Joy in heaven is through the blood because it is the blood that:

   I. Bestows the right to a place in heaven.

  II. Makes us fit for the pleasures in heaven.

 III. Provides subject matter for the song of heaven.

I. It Is the Blood That Bestows on Us the Right to a Place in Heaven.

It is clear that this is the leading thought in the text. To the question "Who are these?" the elder replies that they are people who have "washed their robes and made them white in the blood of the Lamb." That is the one thing to which, as their distinguishing mark, he draws attention. This alone gives them the right to the place which they occupy in glory. This becomes plainly evident if we notice the words which immediately follow: "Therefore they are before the throne of God, and serve Him day and night in His temple. And He who sits on the throne will dwell among them." "Therefore"—it is because of that blood that they are before the throne. They owe it to the blood of the Lamb that they occupy that place so high in glory. *The blood gives the right to heaven.*

Right to heaven! Can such a thing be spoken of in connection with a condemned sinner? Would it not be better to glory only in the mercy of God, who, by free grace, admits a sinner to heaven, than to speak of a *right* to heaven? No, it would not be better—for then we would not understand the value of the blood or why it had to be shed. We might also entertain false conceptions both of our sin and of God's grace, and remain unfit for the full enjoyment of the glorious redemption which the Savior has accomplished for us.

We have already spoken of "the casting out of Satan from heaven," and have shown from this incident that a holy God acts always according to law. Just as the devil was not *cast out* otherwise than according to law and right, so the sinner cannot *be admitted* in any other way. The Prophet Isaiah said, "Zion shall be redeemed with justice, and her penitents with righteousness" (Isaiah 1:27). St. Paul tells us that "grace reigns *through righteousness*" (Romans 5:21). This was the purpose for which God sent His Son into the world. Instead of being afraid that speaking of having a right to enter heaven might *belittle* grace, it will be seen that the highest glory of grace consists in *bestowing* that right.

The lack of this insight is sometimes found in the church where it might be least expected. Recently I asked a man who spoke of the hope he had of going to heaven when he died, on what ground he rested his hope. He was not by any means a careless man nor did he trust to his own righteousness, and yet he replied, "Well, I think that I strive my best to seek the Lord and to do His will." When I told him that this was no ground on which to stand before the judgment seat of a holy God, he appealed to the mercy of God. When I told him again that he needed more than mercy, it appeared to him to be something *new* to hear that it was the righteousness of God only that could grant him entrance into heaven. It is to be feared that there are many who listen to the preaching of "justification by faith" but who have no idea that they cannot have a share in eternal blessedness except by being declared legally righteous.

Entirely different was the testimony of a certain lad who had not the full use of his intellectual faculties but whose heart the Spirit of God had enlightened to understand the meaning of the crucifixion of Jesus.

When on his deathbed he was asked about his hope, he intimated that there was a great book, on one of the pages of which his many sins, very many, had been written. Then with the finger of his right hand he pointed to the palm of his left hand, indicating the print of the nail there. Taking, as it were, something from the pierced hand—he was thinking of the blood that marked it—he showed how all that was written on that page was now blotted out. The blood of the Lamb was the ground of his hope.

The blood of the Lamb gives the believing sinner a right to heaven. "Behold! The Lamb of God who takes away the sin of the world." By shedding His blood He *really* bore the punishment of sin. He gave Himself up to death *really* in our place. He gave His life as a *ransom* for many. Now that the punishment is borne and our Lord's blood has really been shed as a ransom and appears before the throne of God in heaven, now the righteousness of God declares that as the sinner's Surety had fulfilled all the requirements of the law, both as regards punishment and obedience, God pronounces the sinner who believes in Christ to be *righteous*. Faith is just the recognition that Christ has really done *everything* for me; that God's declaration of righteousness is just His declaration that, according to the law and right, I have a title to salvation. God's grace bestows on me the *right* to heaven. The blood of the Lamb is the *evidence* of this right. If I have been cleansed by that blood, I can meet death with full confidence—I have a *right* to heaven.

You desire and hope to get to heaven. Listen then to the answer given to the question, Who are they who will find a place before the throne of God? "They have washed their robes and made them white in the blood of the Lamb." That washing takes place not in heaven and not at death, but here during our life on earth. Do not deceive yourselves by a hope of heaven if you have not been cleansed, really cleansed, by that precious blood. Do not dare to meet death without knowing that Jesus Himself has cleansed you by His blood.

II. The Blood Also Bestows the Fitness for Heaven.

It is of little use for men to have a right to anything unless they are prepared to enjoy it. However costly the gift, it is of little use if the inner attitude necessary to the enjoyment of it is lacking. To bestow the right to heaven on those who are not at the same time prepared for it would give them no pleasure, but would be in conflict with the perfection of all God's works.

The power of the blood of Jesus not only sets open the door of heaven for the sinner but it operates on him in such a divine way that, as he enters heaven, *it will appear that the blessedness of heaven and he have been really fitted for each other.*

What constitutes the blessedness of heaven and what the status is of those who are fitted for it, we are told by words connected with our text. "Therefore they are before the throne of God, and serve Him day and night in His temple. And He who sits on the throne will dwell among them. They shall neither hunger anymore nor thirst anymore; the sun shall not strike them, nor any heat; for the Lamb who is in the midst of the throne will shepherd them and lead them to living fountains of waters. And God will wipe away every tear from their eyes."

Nearness to and fellowship with God and the Lamb consti-

tute the blessedness of heaven. To be before the throne of God
and to see His face, to serve Him day and night in His temple, to
be overshadowed by Him who sits upon the throne, to be
shepherded and led by the Lamb, all these expressions point out
how little the blessedness of heaven depends on anything else
than on *God and the Lamb*. To see Them, to have communion
with Them, to be acknowledged, loved, cared for by Them—
that is blessedness!

What preparation is needed for having such communion with
God and the Lamb? It consists of two things:

(1) Inner agreement in mind and will, and

(2) Delight in His nearness and fellowship. Both are purchased by the blood.

(1) *There can be no thought of fitness for heaven apart from
oneness with God's will.* How could two dwell together unless they
agree? And because God is the holy one, the sinner must be
cleansed from his sin and sanctified. Otherwise he remains utterly unfit for what constitutes the happiness of heaven. "Without holiness no man can see the Lord." Man's entire nature must
be renewed so that he may think and desire and will and do what
pleases God, not as a matter of mere obedience in keeping a commandment but from *natural pleasure, and because he cannot do or
will otherwise. Holiness must become his nature.*

Is not this just what we have seen that the blood of the Lamb
does? "The blood of Jesus Christ His Son cleanses us from all
sin." Where pardon and reconciliation are applied by the Holy
Spirit and are retained by a living faith, there the blood operates
with a divine power, killing sinful lusts and desires. The blood
exercises constantly a wonderful cleansing power. In the blood
the power of the death of Jesus operates: we died with Him to
sin. Through a believing communion with the blood, the power
of the death of Jesus presses into the innermost parts of our hid-

den life. The blood breaks the power of sin and cleanses from all sin.

The blood also sanctifies. We have seen that cleansing is but one part of salvation, the taking away of sin. The blood does more than this: it takes possession of us for God and *inwardly bestows the very same attitude which was in Jesus when He shed His blood.* In shedding that blood He sanctified Himself for us that we also should be sanctified by the truth. As we delight and lose ourselves in that holy blood, the power of entire surrender to God's will and glory—the same power to sacrifice everything to abide in God's love which inspired the Lord Jesus—is efficacious in *us.*

The blood sanctifies us for the emptying and surrender of ourselves so that God may take possession of us and fill us with Himself. This is true holiness: to be possessed by and filled with God. This is wrought by the blood of the Lamb, and so we are prepared here on earth to meet God in heaven with unspeakable joy.

(2) In addition to having one will with God, we said that fitness for heaven consisted in *the desire and capacity for enjoying fellowship with God.* In this, also, the blood bestows, here on earth, the true preparation for heaven. We have seen how the blood brings us near to God, leading to a priestlike approach. Yes, we have liberty by the blood to enter into "the Holiest" of God's presence and to make our dwelling place there. We have seen that God attaches to the blood such incomprehensible value that where the blood is sprinkled, there is His throne of grace. When a heart places itself under the full operation of the blood, there God dwells and there His salvation is experienced. *The blood makes possible the practice of fellowship with God, and also with the Lamb.* Have we forgotten the Savior's statement: "He who eats My flesh and drinks My blood abides in Me, and I in him"? The full bless-

ing of the power of the blood in its highest effect is *full abiding union with Jesus.* It is only our unbelief that separates the work from the person and the blood from the Lord Jesus. It is *He, Himself,* who cleanses by His blood and brings us near and causes us to drink. It is only through the blood that we are fitted for full fellowship with Jesus in heaven, just as with the Father.

You who are redeemed, here you can see what is needed to mold you for heaven, to make you, even here, heavenly minded. See that the blood, which always has a place at the throne of grace above, manifests its power always also in your hearts. Then your lives will become an unbroken fellowship with God and the Lamb—a foretaste of life in eternal glory. Let the thought enter deeply into your soul: the blood bestows already in the heart, here on earth, the blessedness of heaven. The precious blood makes life on earth and life in heaven *one.*

III. The Blood Provides Subject Matter for the Song of Heaven.

What we have hitherto said has been taken from what the heavenly elder stated *about* the redeemed. But how far is this the experience and testimony of the redeemed themselves? Have we anything *out of their own mouths* concerning this? Yes, they themselves bear witness. In the song contained in our text they were heard to cry out with a loud voice, "Salvation belongs to our God who sits on the throne, and to the Lamb!" It is as the slain *Lamb* that the Lord Jesus is in the midst of the throne, as a Lamb whose blood had been shed. *As such,* He is the object of the worship of the redeemed.

This appears still more clearly in the new song that they sing: "You are worthy to take the scroll, and to open its seals; for You were slain, and have redeemed us to God *by Your blood* out of every tribe and tongue and people and nation, and have made us kings and priests unto our God" (Revelation 5:9–10). Or in words somewhat different, those used by the Apostle John in the beginning of the book; there, under the impression of all that he had seen and heard in heaven concerning the place which the Lamb occupied, at the first mention of the name of the Lord Jesus he cried out, "To Him who loved us and *washed us from our sins in His own blood,* and has made us kings and priests to His God and Father, to Him be glory and dominion forever and ever. Amen" (Revelation 1:5–6).

Without ceasing, the blood of the Lamb continues to have power to awaken the saved in heaven to their song of joy and thanksgiving. For His death on the cross was the sacrifice in which He gave Himself for them and won them for Himself. Also, because the blood is the eternal seal of what He did and of the love which moved Him to do it. Therefore it remains the inexhaustible, overflowing fountain of heavenly bliss.

That we may better understand this, notice John's expression: "Him who loved us and washed us from our sins *in His own blood.*" In all our consideration about the blood of Jesus, we have had till now no occasion intentionally to stop there. And of all the glorious things which the blood means, this is one of the most glorious: His blood is the sign, the measure, yes, the impartation of *His love.* Each application of His blood, each time that He causes the soul to experience its power, is a fresh outflowing of His wonderful love! The full experience of the power of the blood in eternity will be nothing else than the full revelation of how He gave Himself up for us *and gives Himself to us* in a love eternal, unending, and as incomprehensible as God Himself.

"Him who loved us and washed us from our sins in His own blood." This love is indeed incomprehensible! What has that love moved Him to do? He gave Himself for us, He became sin for us, He was made a curse for us. Who would dare to use such language, who could ever have dared to think such a thing if God had not revealed it to us by His Spirit? That He really gave Him-

self up for us—not because it was laid upon Him to do so, but by
the impulse of a love that really longed for us, so that we might
forever be identified with Him!

Because it is such a divine wonder, therefore we feel it so
little. But, blessed be the Lord, there is a time coming when we
shall feel it, when under the ceaseless and immediate love-sharing
of the heavenly life we shall be filled and satisfied with that love.
Yes, praise the Lord, even here on earth there is hope that through
a better understanding about and a more perfect trust in the blood,
the love of God will more powerfully be "poured out in our hearts
by the Holy Spirit." There is nothing to prevent our hearts being
filled with the love of the Lamb and our mouths with His praise
here on earth, by faith, as is done in heaven by sight. Each experience of the power of the blood will become increasingly an experience of the love of Jesus.

It has been said that it is not desirable to lay too much emphasis on the word "blood"; that it sounds coarse, and the thought
expressed by it can be conveyed in a way more in accordance
with our modern habit of speaking or thinking.

I must acknowledge that I do not share in this view. I receive
that word as coming not just from John but from the Lord Himself. I am deeply convinced that the word chosen by the Spirit of
God, and by Him made living and so filled with the power of
eternal life that a song containing it comes to us, carries in itself
a power of blessing surpassing our understanding. Changing the
expression into our way of thinking has all the imperfection of a
human translation. He who desires to know and experience "what
the Spirit says to the churches" will accept the word by faith as
having come from heaven—as the word in which joy and power
of eternal life is enfolded in a most distinctive manner. Those
expressions, "*Thy blood*" and "*the blood of the Lamb*," will make
"the Holiest," the place of God's glory, resound eternally with the
joyful notes of the "new song."

Heavenly joy through the blood of the Lamb: that will be the portion of all, here on earth, who with undivided heart yield to its power; and of all above, in heaven, who have become worthy to take a place among the multitude around the throne.

My comrades in redemption, we have learned what those in heaven say and how they sing about the blood. Let us pray earnestly that these tidings may have the effect on us which our Lord intended. We have seen that to live a real heavenly life it is necessary to abide in the full power of the blood. The blood *bestows the right* to enter heaven.

As the *blood of reconciliation* it works out in the soul the full, living consciousness which belongs to those who are "at home" in heaven. It brings us really into "the Holiest," near to God. It *makes us fit* for heaven.

As the *cleansing blood* it delivers from the lust and power of sin and preserves us in the fellowship of the light and life of the holy God. The blood inspires the song of praise in heaven. As the blood of the Lamb "who loved us and gave Himself for us" it speaks not only of *what* He has done for us but chiefly of *Him* who has done all. In the blood we have the most perfect impartation of Himself. He who by faith gives himself up to experience, to the full, what the blood is able to do, will soon find an entrance into a life of happy singing of love and praise that heaven itself, alone, can surpass.

My comrades in redemption, this life is for you and me! *May the blood be all our glory*, not only at the cross with its awful wonders but also at the throne. Let us plunge deep and ever deeper into the living fountain of the blood of the Lamb. Let us open our hearts wide and ever wider for its operation. Let us firmly and ever more firmly believe in the ceaseless cleansing by which the eternal High Priest Himself will apply that blood to us. Let us pray with burning and evermore burning desire that nothing, yes, nothing, may be in our heart that does not experience the power of the blood. Let us unite joyfully in the song of the great multitude who know of nothing so glorious as this: "You have redeemed us to God by your blood."

May our life on earth become what it ought to be, O our beloved Lord: *one ceaseless song* to "Him who loved us and washed us from our sins in His own blood, and has made us kings and priests to His God and Father"!

"To Him be the glory and dominion forever and ever." Amen.

Book II

The Blood of the Cross

Preface

IN HIS preface to the Dutch Edition of this volume, the late Rev. Andrew Murray, M.A., D.D., tells us that while on a journey to Europe his mind was directed definitely to the consideration of the "power of the blood of Jesus." That phrase gripped him and seemed to keep demanding from him, "What does the power of the blood really mean?" He says, "My consideration of this question, and my meditation upon the Scriptures to find an answer to it, was made a great blessing to me." On his return to South Africa, he took up this subject for consideration during Passion Week with his congregation in Wellington. Fifteen addresses were delivered on that occasion, then five at a later date. (The substance of the first ten of these discourses has already been published in the book *The Power of the Blood of Jesus*; the remaining ten are now sent forth in this companion volume, *The Blood of the Cross*.)

He published them, he says, "because I am deeply convinced that we Christians can never know too much about the truths which the blood proclaims. There can be no freedom of approach to God, nor fellowship with Him, apart from a truly vital and powerful experience of the efficacy of the blood of Christ. Its efficacy is a hidden, spiritual, divine reality, and therefore can be experienced only in a heart that is humbly and entirely submitted to the guidance of the Spirit of God. And to whatever degree we have an insight into the disposition that inspired Christ to shed His blood, we shall also understand and experience what that power is which can produce that disposition in us.

"Reconciliation and deliverance from guilt will become the blessed entrance for us into a life in which Christ's blood—as it was translated into heaven and abides there—will be truly the power of a divine abiding life in us.

"It is not without hesitancy that I publish these meditations. There is always the danger, when one attempts to explain divine mysteries in human words, of leading souls away from the one thing that can bring blessing to them, namely, waiting on God for His Spirit to reveal these truths. I have endeavored to remember that just as the blood is the deepest mystery of redemption, so its power can be experienced only with a mental outlook akin to that of Him who shed it.

"I cherish the hope that, for those who read these addresses with that disposition, they may be a help and blessing to them; and that they may long be kept engaged in the consideration from every standpoint of what is in truth the center of God's wondrous counsel of redemption. It is my prayer that the Lord our God may lead all His people, and me also, ever deeper into the blessed experience of a heart and daily walk in which the blood manifests its power, and into a fellowship with God in the liberty and intimacy which the blood can bring about. May He cause us to experience and manifest what it means to say that we have 'washed our garments and made them white in the blood of the Lamb.' So may it be."

WM. M. DOUGLAS
Middelburg,
Union of South Africa.

Contents

1

"When I See the Blood"

"Now the blood shall be a sign for you on the houses where you are. And when I see the blood, I will pass over you; and the plague shall not be on you to destroy you when I strike the land of Egypt."—Exodus 12:13.

THE story of the Passover is well-known to us all.
The Lord was about to lead His people out of Egypt and, on the night of their departure, to inflict judgment upon Egypt. The Lord considered Israel as His firstborn son among the nations. Egypt had transgressed against Him by ill treatment of this firstborn son, and so punishment was to fall on "the firstborn" of Egypt. In every house the firstborn would be smitten by the destroying angel, who, at midnight, would pass through the land of Egypt.

The Egyptians and Israelites in many cases dwelt near one another, and so a sign must be set on the door of every Israelitish house, that the destroying angel might not enter there to slay. That sign was to be the blood of a lamb, slain by the father of the family, according to the commandment given by God. "The blood shall be a sign for you"—so God had said. It was to be a sign, an assurance by which the Israelite might have entire confidence concerning the safety of his family. It would be a sign also before God, of the disposition of the father of the house—regarding his obedience of faith—through which God would spare his house:

"When I see the blood, I will pass over you."

We know why it is that the blood, and nothing else, was established by God as a sign. Although Israel was God's people, they were also, alas, a sinful people. As far as sin was concerned, if Israel was to be treated as they deserved, then the destroying angel must exercise judgment on them also. But the blood was to be a token of redemption. The death of the lamb that was slain was considered as taking the place of the death which each first-born Israelite had earned by his sin. The redemption of Israel, however, was not to take place simply by the exercise of power, but in accord with law and righteousness. Therefore, in each Israelitish home the punishment of sin had to be warded off by the blood of the paschal lamb. Each father of a household, by the sprinkling of blood around the door of his house, had to give proof of his recognition of his sinfulness and need of deliverance, and of his confidence in God's promise of redemption, by his willing obedience to God's command. All this was in a remarkable way represented by the blood of the paschal lamb.

In the New Testament we read: "Christ, our Passover, was sacrificed for us." The outstanding name which He bears in heaven, *i.e.,* the Lamb of God, refers chiefly to what He, as our paschal lamb, has done for our redemption. And if we wish to declare in the most simple manner how His blood obtains our salvation, then we cannot teach it in a better way than by this figure or type—the Passover in Egypt.

Later on, in subsequent chapters, we shall go much more into depth in explaining the power of Jesus' blood to mature believers. We now address ourselves to the simplest and most unlearned in spiritual things, to those who as yet may understand nothing about this blood. May God grant to them a knowledge of the preciousness of the blood of Christ by the glorious type supplied by the Passover!

Let our attention be drawn to:

I. The danger to be averted by the blood.

II. The deliverance which is effected by the blood.

III. The blessings we may obtain by the blood.

I. The Danger to Be Averted by the Blood.

There are four facts at which I would like us to look. One, the danger was awful; the Eternal God was about to send the destroying angel with his sword through the land. Two, it was general; no house was to be spared. Each family was to be robbed of its crown: the firstborn must die. Three, it was certain; no power of man could procure redemption. Four, it was unexpected.

All of these truths have application to the present. We have here a terrible picture of the danger that threatens us, and from which there is no deliverance except by the blood of the Lamb.

The danger is awful. This was true of Egypt, and it is true now: a hiding place, a means of redemption, has no value if the danger is not realized. The blood of Jesus, however precious it is in the eyes of God and of the redeemed, has no value for him who has not realized his danger. The world is under the wrath of God. However happily life is spent, however we boast about our present civilization and prosperity and progress, there hangs over this world a heavy, dark cloud, more terrible than that which hung over Egypt. There is a day of judgment approaching, when anger and wrath, tribulation and anguish shall be recompensed for all disobedience and sin. Christ shall appear in flaming fire, taking vengeance on those who "do not know God, and on those who do not obey the gospel" (2 Thess. 1:8). He will pronounce the terrible sentence upon all who do not belong to Him: "Depart from Me, you cursed, into the everlasting fire prepared for the devil and his angels." We have been warned: "For behold, the day is coming, burning like an oven, . . . and who can stand when He appears?" (Mal. 4:1, 3:2).

The danger is general. No house in Egypt was to be passed by. From the palace of the king to the hut of the beggar, the firstborn had to die. There was no distinction. Rich and poor, fashionable and ill-bred, friends and enemies of Israel, those who were kind, as well as the most cruel oppressors of the people—that night there was no difference between them. The nation had sinned; the judgment must come upon all, without exception.

It will be just the same with the judgment which is one day coming upon the world. We all have sinned; we are all under a curse and God's wrath. No one—unless God Himself in a miraculous manner has redeemed him—will escape this unendurable judgment. No reader of these words, whoever he is, can escape standing before God's throne—to be cast then into the outer darkness on account of his sins, if God's mercy has not accomplished for him a miracle of grace.

The danger is certain. We are living in the days of which Scripture has spoken, when scoffers, walking after their own lusts, say: "Where is the promise of His coming? For all things continue as they were from the beginning of the creation." God is longsuffering, and extends the days of grace, but the day of judgment will surely come. No power or force, no wisdom or cunning, no riches or honor can enable man to escape it. It comes certainly. As surely as there is a God in heaven who is a righteous judge, as surely as there is sin on earth opposed to God's holy law, as surely as there is in every child of man consciousness that sin must be punished by a judge, so surely that day will come. Although the thought of the millions who then will be lost, and of the terribleness of the breaking loose of the pent-up fire of God's wrath, and of the misery of an eternal separation from God's presence is too terrible to rightly apprehend or bear—it is true and certain. There hangs over the whole world, and over every soul, a dark cloud of the wrath of God, which will speedily break loose and burn with a fire that through eternity will not be extinguished.

The danger is unexpected. In Egypt they were busy buying and selling, building and trading, living luxuriously and boasting about their power and wisdom; but in one night the whole land was plunged into the deepest sorrow. "So Pharaoh rose in the night, he, all his servants, and all the Egyptians; and there was a great cry in Egypt." It was in Egypt as in the days of the flood, and of Sodom and Gomorrah: in an hour when they thought not, the angel of destruction came.

So will it ever be. The devil lulls men to sleep by the busyness and enjoyments of this world; but death comes—unexpected. Judgment comes—unexpected. While one still puts matters off to a more convenient season, while another comforts himself with the assurance that he will yet sometime be delivered, while still others do not trouble themselves at all about these things—judgment ever draws nearer. It has happened more than once that a man has fallen asleep on the railroad track; everything around him seemed restful and still; suddenly the express train came rushing on, and crushed him to death.

God's judgment draws near with incomprehensible rapidity and power. Because everything around you is quiet and safe and appears joyous, I beseech you, do not deceive yourselves. Judgment comes unexpectedly, and then—then it is forever too late. Believe this, I beg you: the danger is greater and nearer than you imagine. Make haste to be delivered.

II. The Deliverance Which Is Effected by the Blood.

Deliverance is planned by God Himself. Let this be a settled conviction with you, that no human wisdom is of any avail here. It is from God's judgment, which is so terrible and irresistible, that we must flee. It is God alone who can point out the way of escape. Deliverance by the blood of a lamb was the outcome of divine wisdom, and if a sinner desires to be delivered, then he must learn in this matter to be entirely submissive to God and entirely dependent upon Him. He must see that he has to deal with what is really a divine purpose, and that, as sure and powerful as the destruction is, just so sure and powerful is the deliverance which has been prepared for him.

Deliverance is through substitution. That was the meaning of the blood of the slaughtered paschal lamb. The Israelite was just as sinful as the Egyptian. If the destroying angel came, he would have the right—yes (if an angel must go by right) it would be his *duty* to enter each house of Israel. But if on the door of the Israelite he found the blood . . . ah, what does that signify?

When the Israelite took the lamb and raised the knife to slay that innocent creature for the sake of its blood, which he had need of for his deliverance, he had only one thought in his mind: "I am sinful; my house is sinful; and the angel of God's wrath is coming tonight. If he acts according to what I deserve, then death will enter my house. But I offer this lamb to die for me and my house." That word "for me"—"in my place"—was the one thought in his heart.

This lamb served as a type: "God will provide for Himself the lamb." The Lord has done this. He has—oh, wonder of wonders!—given His own Son to die in our place. The death which Jesus died was my death. He bore my sins. I need not now die. The deliverance which God has prepared is through substitution. Jesus, my substitute, has paid all—all my indebtedness to God's law—and has done everything for me. He has entirely broken the power of sin and death, and I can now, at once, be entirely acquitted and be freed from all my sins. Deliverance is through substitution.

Deliverance is by means of the sprinkling of blood. The blood of the lamb had to be sprinkled on the lintel and the two doorposts. It was not enough that the lamb should be slain and its blood shed; the blood must be personally applied. The father of the family had to take the blood and sprinkle it on the doorframe of his house. And so the Scripture says that our conscience must be cleansed, and our heart must be sprinkled. "Let us draw near . . . having our hearts sprinkled from an evil conscience" (Heb. 10:22).

In this deliverance, God and man meet one another; each has his share in the work. God provided the Lamb—His own Son. God, through the eternal Spirit, prepared Him to be a sacrifice. God promised to accept the blood. God bestows upon us, by the blood, justification, cleansing, and sanctification. All this is the work of God. Our work is to believe in that blood, and in faith to submit ourselves to the sprinkling of it. The result is real and eternal.

Deliverance is through the obedience of faith. For the Israelite it was a new and hitherto unheard-of thing, that the destroying angel was to come, and that the blood on the doorframe—roughly in the form of a cross—would deliver him. But he believed God's word, and in that belief he did what he had been commanded. This is just what you have to do, you who are longing for deliverance from eternal death. Exercise faith in the blood; be assured that if God tells you the blood of His Son cleanses you from all sin, that it is the truth. The blood has a supernatural, heavenly, divine power, to cover and blot out sin before God immediately and forever. Accept this as God's truth, and rest upon it. Then be obedient, and appropriate that blood which accomplishes such wonders. Reckon that it was shed for you; humble yourself before God, that the Holy Spirit may apply it to you, and cleanse your heart by it. Simply believe in that blood as shed for you. The Almighty God is faithful, and will accept you for the sake of the blood. Jesus will cleanse you by His blood and will work out in you the cleansing, and impart to you the joy and the power which the blood alone can bestow.

The blood effects an immediate deliverance from the judgment of God. The blood delivered the Israelites immediately and entirely from the threatened danger of that night. In the same way, from the moment that you are sprinkled by that blood, you are justified from your sins, and the judgment of God is averted from you. This blessing is so great, so divine, that it appears to man too great to be true. We desire to see in ourselves some token of improvement, to feel something as a proof that God has received us. It seems incredible that God could thus justify the unrighteous immediately; and yet it is so.

This is the divine glory of redemption through the blood of the Lamb. This blood has such a divine and life-giving power that the moment a man believes in it, he is cleansed from all his sins. You who desire to be saved from sin and judgment may rely upon this. The blood effects an immediate redemption. The blood is so unspeakably precious to God, as the proof of the obedience of His Son, that God, for His Son's sake and because of His pleasure in Him, immediately forgives and receives you, if only you trust in that blood.

The blood is the beginning of a new life. You know that the Feast of Unleavened Bread was closely connected with the Feast of the Passover. When leaven was used, it came from a portion of an old lump of dough used in a previous baking. Leavening is a process of corruption. Israel had to use unleavened bread during the Passover Feast and the seven following days, as a proof that they would no longer have anything to do with the old leaven of Egypt; everything must become entirely new. The sprinkling with the blood of Christ is the commencement of an entirely new life.

The blood and the Spirit of Christ are inseparable. When the sinner is brought near to God by the blood, he is renewed and sanctified by the Spirit. The blood is the beginning and pledge of a life in the service of God.

The blood gives assurance of the love and guidance of God. Israel was delivered by the sprinkling of the blood from the power of the destroying angel, and also from the power of Pharaoh. The Red Sea, the pursuit by Pharaoh, the trials of the desert—these were still to come; but the blood was the pledge that God would be responsible for everything. The blood of Christ gives you a share in the love, the guidance, and the protection of God. Oh, if you only understood this: the God who has provided the blood of His Son, who has received you because of that blood—He has become your God. He who has given His Son for you, how shall He not with Him also freely give you all things? This is the blessing and power of the blood—it brings you into an eternal covenant with God. He becomes your leader and your portion.

The blood is the pledge of a perfect redemption. The God who delivered Israel from Egypt by the blood was not satisfied until He had brought Israel into Canaan. And God bestows upon you not only the blood of Christ, but the living Christ Himself. Because He ever lives, He can save to the uttermost. Each moment of your life He will care for you. He undertakes to provide for every weakness and need. He will, here in this life, lead you into the full blessedness of God's love. He becomes surety for your arrival in eternal glory. His blood is the eternal and undeniable proof that all God the Father and Christ see needful They will do, and that They will not forsake you; They will accomplish Their work in you from beginning to end. All the blessedness and all the glory of redemption are securely founded on the precious blood. Oh, you who up till now have had no part in that blood, let me persuade you to seek for salvation in the blood of the Lamb of God. Do not rest until you have the assurance, the perfect certainty, of your redemption.

III. The Blessings We May Obtain by the Blood

When the Israelite had sprinkled the blood he knew that he was safe. God had given him a promise of protection, and he was able trustfully to await the terrible visit of the destroying angel. He could listen peacefully to the great cry in the streets around him. His safety lay in God, who had said: "When I see the blood, I will pass over you."

How much more may we, who now have not the blood of an earthly lamb but that of the Lamb of God from heaven—how much more may we be assured of our redemption! You who read this, give, I pray you, an answer to the question I now ask: Have you this assurance? Are you truly sheltered from the day of wrath, under the protection of the blood? Have you the assurance that you also have been redeemed by that blood? If not, hasten, without delay, to receive this blessing. The danger is so terrible. The redemption is so glorious; the conditions are so full of grace. Let nothing keep you back from obtaining a share in it. You must be sure about it, or you will have no rest for your soul.

It is recorded that on the Passover night there was an old gray-haired man who lived in the house of his firstborn son; and he himself was the firstborn son of his father. His son also had a firstborn son. Thus there were three firstborn sons in the house, who all must die if the destroying angel entered the house. The old man was lying on his bed, sick, but he heard with interest everything his son told him about God's command to Moses. Towards evening he was often restless, as he thought of their danger, and he said: "My son, are you sure that you have done everything that has been prescribed?" The answer was: "Yes, Father, everything." For a moment he was satisfied. Then he asked again:

"Are you sure? Has the blood been sprinkled around the door?" Again the answer was: "Yes, Father, everything has been done according to the command." The nearer it came to midnight, the more restless he became. Finally he cried out: "My son, carry me out if you please, that I myself may see it, and then I can rest." The son took his father up, and carried him to where he could see the blood on the side posts and the lintel. "Now I am satisfied," cried he. "Thank God! Now I know that I am safe!"

My reader, can you say that? Can you say, "Thank God, now I know that I am safe. I know that the blood was shed for me and has been sprinkled on me"? If not, I beseech you, by the terror and certainty of the judgment of God, make haste this day to hearken to God's command. Turn away from your sin, and place your trust in the blood. Oh, I pray you, add not now to all your other sins that of despising, rejecting, treading upon the blood of the Son of God! I beseech you by the mercy of God, and the wondrous love of the Son of God, flee from the wrath to come, and seek for shelter under the blood which alone can redeem. Believe, I beseech you, that no prayer, no worship, no works, no endeavor will avail you anything. But God has said: "When I see the blood, I will pass over you." Let that be your confidence. If He does not see the blood on me, He will not spare me. Come *now,* today, to this dear Savior, who lives to cleanse you with His blood, and who never once has rejected anyone who came to Him.

2

Redeemed to God by the Blood

"You are worthy . . . for You were slain, and have redeemed us to God by Your blood"—Revelation 5:9.

"REDEEMED"—"bought": that word is understood by everybody. Commerce occupies a great place in our lives. We are all so constantly engaged in buying or selling that the ideas attached to them are understood by everybody. The right that the buyer obtains over that which previously had not been his; the value which he attaches to it after its price has been paid; the certainty that what he has bought will be given to him; and the use that he will make of his purchase—all these things are obvious, and daily, in a thousand ways, they affect the life of the community.

The words of our text, taken from a heavenly hymn of praise, "You have redeemed us to God by Your blood," invite us to see in the mirror of earthly trade what "the blood of the Lamb" has done for us, and what a clear knowledge of this fact entails. The right that our Lord Jesus, "the Lamb of God," has obtained for us, and the claim that we now have in regard to Him; what we may expect from Him, and what He expects from us—all these things will become plain to us. If the Holy Spirit teaches us to regard the blood in the light of these resemblances, our hearts surely will take up the song of heaven with new joy: "You are worthy . . . for You were slain, and have redeemed us to God by Your blood."

Following these thoughts, let us notice:

I.   The right to us which He has obtained.
II. The claim which He makes upon us.
III. The joy with which He will receive us.
IV. The certainty that He will protect and care for us.

I. The Right to Us Which He Has Obtained.

"You have redeemed us to God by Your blood"—that indicates the right which He has obtained to possess us and control us. As Creator, the Lord Jesus has a right to every soul of man. Through Him God has bestowed life upon men, that they might be His possession and inheritance. Never on earth has any maker had such a right over his own work as Jesus has over us. We belong to Him.

Consider what this classic statement declares: "It has often happened among men that one has had to buy back what really belonged to him, but which had been taken from him by a hostile power. Many times a people has had to buy back their land and freedom by their blood. After that, land and liberty become of increased value."

Thus, the Son of God has ransomed us from the power of Satan. God, at creation, had placed man under the government of His Son. By yielding to the temptations of Satan, man fell from God, and became entirely subject to the authority of the tempter. Man became Satan's slave. It was the law of God that prohibited sin and threatened punishment. When man sinned, it was also this law that bestowed upon Satan his authority. God had said: "In the day that you eat from that tree, you will fall into the grip of death." And our original parents disobeyed. So God gave man up to be a slave in the prison house of Satan. And for man there was no possibility of redemption except by ransom—by the payment of the price which the law righteously demands for the redemption of prisoners.

You know that word "redemption." In old times, when it was the custom that prisoners of war should be made slaves, sometimes a very high price was paid by the friends or rulers of the prisoners as ransom for their deliverance from slavery. Jesus Christ has purchased, with His own blood, our freedom from the prison and slavery of Satan in which he as our enemy had lodged us, and to which the law of God had condemned us.

To purchase, to ransom, means always that one valuable thing is given for another. Our souls needed redemption: the law demanded the payment of a ransom. We were under its power and condemnation. We were held as prisoners until what we owed was paid, a recompense for the wrongs we had done—the requirement, a perfect righteousness. Jesus came and gave Himself in our place, His soul for our soul. He bore our punishment of death, our curse of death; He shed His blood as reconciliation for our sin. That blood was the ransom price by which we are redeemed. He gave His life for our life, and His blood gave Him an eternal right to us. And now the message comes to us as from heaven: Jesus has bought us by His blood; He and none else has a right to us. Not Satan, not the world, not ourselves, have any right to us. The Son of God has bought us with His blood; He *only* has a right to us. We belong to *Him.*

Oh, my reader, be still and listen, and recognize that right. Perhaps you have never known this, or have never meditated upon it. An eternal price has been paid for you. A price has been paid for you of more value than the whole world—the blood of God's Son. You have been redeemed from the power of Satan; God proclaims you to be *now* the possession of His Son. And the Son comes today to take possession of what belongs to Him. He asks you, "Do you know that you belong to Me? Will you recognize My right?" His blood, His love, God as judge, the law as creditor, Satan as jailer—all agree. The Lord who has redeemed you by His blood has a right to you. Oh, let your heart respond:

"Yes, Lord, I acknowledge that You, and You alone, have a right to me."

II. The Claim Which He Makes upon Us.

"You have redeemed us to God by Your blood." These words remind us of the claim which He makes on us. A person may have a right to something without exercising that right; he lays no claim to it. But it is not thus with Jesus Christ. He comes to us with the urgent request that we should surrender ourselves to Him. You know how, in every ordinary purchase, the buyer has the right to ask that what he has purchased shall be given to him; it is carefully stated when and where the delivery will take place. Jesus Christ sends His servants with the request that *without delay*, at the hour and in the place where the message is delivered, *there* the persons, as His purchased possession, should hand themselves over and become subject to Him. That message comes to you again today. He entreats you to say farewell to all foreign authority that has ruled over you and to become His sole possession.

Chief among those foreign powers is sin. By our descent from fallen Adam, sin has a terrible, irresistible authority over us. It has soaked to the deepest roots of our nature; it is thoroughly at home in us; it has *become* our nature. However strongly we may be inclined—either by the voice of God, or by conscience, or by the sense of misery which sin has produced in us, or by some desire after good which may be awakened in us to forsake the service of sin—*sin refuses to release us*. As slaves of sin, we have no power to break the bonds which bind us. But Jesus, who has bought us by His blood, now calls upon us to give ourselves to Him. However deeply we experience that we have been sold under sin, and that the law of sin always holds us prisoners, He promises to deliver us from its tyranny, and that He will Himself bestow upon us the power to serve and follow Him as Lord. He asks only for the choice of our hearts, the honest declaration of our wills—that we recognize His right and yield ourselves to Him. He will see to it that the authority of sin shall be destroyed.

Another of the foreign powers which has exercised authority over us is the world. The needs and business of the world are so manifold and so urgent; they lay claim to our lives and all our powers. The promises, the enjoyments, the temptations which the world presents to us are so flattering, and exercise such an unconscious influence upon us, that it is impossible for us of ourselves to offer resistance to them. The favor and assistance of the people we associate with, and their displeasure and contempt if we separate ourselves from them to live only for God, induce in many an enslavement to the world. It rules over them, and demands their obedience. Satan is the ruler of this world, and through it exercises his power over them. Jesus Christ comes as conqueror of Satan and the world, and asks us to choose which we wish to serve—Him, or this enemy of His. He asks this of us, as those who belong to Him. He points us to His blood, to the right to us which He has obtained, and asks that we should recognize this right and surrender ourselves as His possession.

There is another power, a still stronger one, foreign and hostile to Christ. It is the power of "self." It is here that sin has produced its most terrible ruin. The doing of our own will, seeking our own pleasure and our own honor, are so deeply rooted in us that apart from an entire revolution it can never be otherwise. Body and soul, understanding and imagination, inclination and love—all are subject to the terrible power of self-pleasing, to the tyranny of "self." Jesus Christ asks that "self" should be pulled down from the throne, and condemned to death. He asks that in all things His will and not ours should be supreme. He beseeches us to make an end of slavery to other lords, and to give ourselves up to Him as His purchased possession.

Each of us must deal with this claim, this request by "the

Lamb of God." How you deal with it will decide what your life will be in time and in eternity. A voice comes to us from heaven, saying: "He is worthy; He has been slain; He has redeemed us to God by His blood." Oh, that our hearts might no longer hesitate, but by faith in that divine blood might respond to His call and reply: "You are worthy, O Lord! Here I am; take what You have purchased. I yield myself to You as Your possession."

III. The Joy with Which He Will Receive Us.

"You have redeemed us to God by Your blood"—that gives us the pledge of the joy with which He will receive us. When a sinner has been urged to give himself to the Lord, and he declares his willingness to do so, he is, alas, often hindered by the fear that he is unworthy to be received. He feels himself so sinful, so dead. He feels he is greatly lacking in humility and real earnestness, and in that heartfelt love which befits one who desires to give himself to such a Lord; therefore he cannot believe the Lord will receive him so instantly, so fully and so eternally. He cannot understand it. Still less does he feel in his heart that it is true.

What a glorious answer to all these questionings is in this word: "You have redeemed us to God by Your blood." Do you not know that if a person buys anything he will surely take possession of it, especially if it is delivered to him? You have, I suppose, sometime bought something? As you have paid your money for it and it was given or brought to you, were you not willing to receive it and take possession of it? The higher the price you paid for it, the less was there any doubt that you would take possesssion of what you had paid for.

"But"—you will perhaps answer—"if I buy something, I know what it is, and that it is worth the price I paid. But I, with my sinful heart, with everything so dead and miserable—there is good reason for me to fear that He who purchased me will not receive me. I am not what I ought to be. When I buy an article and another of less worth is sent to me, I refuse to receive it. I send it back with the message: 'This is not what I bought and for which I have paid.'"

You are right, but consider what the difference is between Him who has bought us by His blood and mere human purchasers. He bought what He *knew* was bad—*because* it was bad; and He will accept it so that His love may have the joy and glory of making it *good*. How wonderful this is! It is nevertheless true. The worse you are, and the deeper you have sunk in the helplessness of your sin, the more fit you are for Him. The Scripture says: "Christ died for the ungodly; while we were yet sinners, Christ died for us." It says, further, that the price of Christ's blood was paid for those who denied the Lord, for those who sold Him, and even for His rejecters. Understand, I pray you, that Jesus has paid an eternal price for you—though you are one who is an enemy, one who is a lawful slave of Satan, one who is entirely dead in sin. He comes to you who are in this condition with the request that you surrender yourself to Him, and with the promise that He will receive you just as you are.

I beseech you, do not any longer allow yourself to be kept by Satan from your Lord and Savior. It is Satan who whispers to you that you are too unworthy, that mercy is not for you because you are so sinful. It is a lie—a lie born in hell! Yes, you are *utterly* unworthy, but not *too* unworthy; for mercy is only for unworthy persons. If you have no desire to serve this Lord, if His love and His blood have no value in your eyes, say so openly, and refuse to give yourself to Him as His purchased property; but if your heart acknowledges that you by right belong to Him—oh, come, I beg you, and believe that He will receive you instantly. And let every doubt depart under the power of that one declaration: "You have redeemed me by Your blood."

It is impossible for the Lord Jesus to refuse to receive you. Between Him and the Father there is an eternal covenant concerning you. The Father has, righteously, given Him right and authority over you; and Jesus has paid your ransom at the great price that has freed you from the tyranny of Satan. He has been constantly calling you to come to Him. He now entreats you again to give yourself up to Him. How can you be so foolish as to think that He will not receive you? Then doubt no longer. Although you are devoid of feeling, and everything appears cold and dead, come and cast yourself down before Him, and say to Him that as He has bought you, you rely upon Him to receive you. He will certainly do so.

IV. The Certainty That He Will Protect and Care for Us.

"You have redeemed us to God by Your blood." This assures us that He will preserve us and care for us. The man who has purchased something of value—for instance, a good horse—not only receives it when it is brought to him, but he appreciates it, he takes care of it and provides for it. He exercises it. He does all this that he may have the utmost service and pleasure out of it. When Jesus Christ receives us—however glorious that is!—it is only the beginning. We can rely on Him who bought us by His blood to complete His work in us.

It is just the lack of insight into this truth that holds many troubled persons back from surrender, and causes many of weak faith to live always in trouble and worry. They do not apply to spiritual things what they understand so well in earthly affairs. When a man has paid a high price for something, even if only a horse or a sheep, he takes it for granted that he must care for it in order that he may have pleasure and service from it. And the Lord Jesus—how is it that you do not understand it?—takes upon Himself to care for you, and so to order things that He may attain His purpose in you. You cannot guard yourself against temptation or going astray. You cannot manage yourself or make yourself fit for His service. You cannot direct yourself so that you may know how to act in everything according to His will and that of the Father. *You* cannot do it. But *He* can! He will, as the One who has bought you with His blood.

My fellow believer, the right that the Lord Jesus has obtained for you is so infinitely high, so broad, so unlimited, that if you will only think about it, you will respond to it. Just as I desire that every member of my body—the eye, the ear, the hand, the foot—should always be at my service, so the Lord desires that you, as a member of His body, along with every power and faculty, should always, without a moment's break, serve Him. You are so far from being able to do this that you may not even realize the possibility of it. Cease trying to do it on your own, and begin each day by committing yourself to the almighty keeping and control of your Lord. Just as a horse or a sheep with each new day must be afresh cared for by its owner, even more so must you, as the property of the Son of God, be cared for by Him. Christ is not an owner who is *outside* of you, or who is only in heaven above; He is *your Head,* and just as the first Adam lives within you with his sinful nature, so He as the Second Adam *lives in you* with His holy nature and by His Holy Spirit. And the one thing to which He calls you is to trust Him, to wait for Him, to rely confidently upon Him to complete in the outward things of our lives His hidden and unnoticed work of protection and perfection. Would that each one of us might know what is implied by our being accepted as the blood-bought possession of Jesus.

It implies that:

He has set a very high value upon us, and so He will not allow any evil to befall us. He will manifest His love to us. He has need of us for His work and glory, and it is His desire and joy to adorn us with His salvation, and to fill us with His unspeakable joy. Meditate upon this till it becomes fixed firmly in your mind.

Our great need is to recognize ourselves as His possession, and by a reverent confession of this to have the heart filled by the consciousness of it. Just as a faithful dog often shows so great attachment to his owner that he will not cease following him, let the wonderful ownership of Jesus, His blood-bought right, so possess you that it will every moment be the keynote of your life, and the power of an enduring attachment to Him.

We should cultivate trust in Him, and let it completely control our whole soul and every thought as to how we are to spend our life and do our work. A possession is preserved and cared for by the owner. Jesus, my heavenly and almighty Owner, who has bought me for Himself by His blood, and prizes me as "the dear purchase" of that blood—He will surely protect me; He will surely fit me for all things in which He intends to make use of me.

"You are worthy, for You were slain, and have redeemed us to God by Your blood." Oh, my readers, listen, I pray you, to the song of heaven, and let it begin to sound in your heart. Let it be the heart confession of your relationship to the slain Lamb. Remember, I pray you, that the blood is the power of salvation, and the subject of heavenly praise. Remember that the blood is the power that binds us to Jesus in bonds that cannot be loosened.

Let him who has not yet acknowledged the claim of Christ do so today, and let him now say: "You are worthy; for the sake of Your blood You shall have me."

Let him who has already acknowledged the Lord's claim abandon himself to the heavenly influences of the Holy Spirit for the destruction of all doubt and slowness of heart, and for the enduement of power to live wholly for the Lamb of God.

Meditate upon and adore God because of this divine wonder, that you have been bought by the blood of the Son of God, and let your life become a translation into earthly walk and behavior which will agree with the song: "You are worthy, for You were slain, and have redeemed us to God by Your blood."

3

The Spirit and the Blood

A Pentecost Message

"And there are three who bear witness on earth: the Spirit, the water, and the blood; and these three agree as one."—1 John 5:8.

I WISH to consider a few of the glorious things which the blood of Christ accomplishes in us—*i.e.*, its blessings. But as we look into this matter, an objection may arise that it is difficult for us to enjoy these blessings. This is because we do not clearly understand what those accomplishments are or how the blood produces them. Or even if we do in some measure understand, it is because it is not possible for us always to experience the blood's power, for we cannot always actively cooperate with it. Such difficulties often arise because we do not remember that God has provided that the blood, as a vital power, automatically and ceaselessly carries on towards perfection its work within us. He has so inseparably bound together the Holy Spirit and the blood that we may surely rely on Him to make ceaselessly efficacious in us, through the Spirit, the blessed power of the blood.

This is the thought expressed in our text. The Apostle John had in the previous verses (4 and 5) spoken about faith in Jesus, and then he directs attention to the testimony on which that faith rests (verses 8–11). He mentions three witnesses:

The Water. This refers to an outward and human act, commanded by God to be observed by those who, turning from their sins, presented themselves to Him: baptism.

The Blood. In this element we see what God has done to bring about a real and living cleansing.

The Spirit. By the Holy Spirit the witness of both the others is confirmed.

In this chapter we shall confine our attention to the truth that the united witness of the Spirit and the blood is the foundation of our faith.

Let us notice the unbroken union of these two witnesses:

    I. In the work of redemption.

   II. In our personal experience.

I. The Union of the Spirit and the Blood in the Work of Redemption.

It is through the Spirit alone that the blood has its efficacy and power; attention to this is foremost. We read in the Epistle to the Hebrews (9:14): "How much more shall the blood of Christ, who through the eternal Spirit offered Himself without spot to God, purge your conscience from dead works to serve the living God." The blood possesses its power to cleanse and to make us fit to serve the living God because of the eternal Spirit, who was in our Lord when He shed His blood. This does not mean merely that the Holy Spirit was in the Lord Jesus and bestowed on His person and His blood a divine worth. It is much more than that—it indicates that the shedding of His blood was *brought about by* the eternal Spirit, and that the Spirit lived and worked in that blood, so that when it was shed it could not decay as a dead thing, but as a living reality it could be taken up to heaven to exercise its divine power from there.

It is expressly for this reason that the Spirit is here called "the eternal Spirit." "Eternal" is one of the words of Scripture which everyone thinks he understands, but there are few who realize what a deep and glorious meaning it has. It is supposed that "eternal" speaks of something that always continues, something that has no end. This explanation is a merely negative one and tells us only what "eternal" is not; it teaches us nothing about its nature and being. Everything that exists in time has a beginning and is subject to the law of increase and decrease, of becoming and decaying. But what is eternal has no beginning and knows no change or weakening, because it has in itself a life that is independent of time. In what is eternal there is no past which has already disappeared and is lost, and there is no future not yet possessed. There is always a glorious and endless present.

Now, when Scripture speaks of "eternal" life, "eternal" redemption, "eternal" joy, it means much more than to say that merely they will have no end. By that word we are taught that the person who has a share in eternal blessedness possesses something in which the power of an endless life is at work, something in which there can be no change, nor can it suffer any diminution. It is something which, therefore, we may always enjoy in the fullness of its life-bestowing blessing.

The object of Scripture in using that word is to teach us that if our faith lays hold on what is eternal, it will manifest itself in us as a power superior to all the changeableness of our mind or feelings, with a youthfulness which never grows old and a freshness which does not for a moment wither.

From this verse we are also taught something about the blood of Jesus—"Who through the eternal Spirit offered Himself without spot to God." Not only had the act of shedding His blood an eternally availing worth, the blood itself has Spirit and life in it, and is always efficacious by the power of an eternal life. This is why the Epistle to the Hebrews lays so much emphasis on the work of Christ as being once for all, and eternal. Notice the expressions in chapter 7: He is "a priest forever according to the order of Melchizedek"; His ministry is based on "the power of an endless life"; He has an "unchangable priesthood"; "Therefore

He is also able to save to the uttermost those who come to God through Him, since He ever lives to make intercession for them"; He is "the Son who has been perfected forever" (verses 17, 16, 24, 25, 28). Further on we read (in 9:12): "with His own blood He entered the Most Holy Place once for all, having obtained eternal redemption"; and in 10:14: "By one offering He has perfected forever those who are being sanctified." It speaks also of "the blood of the everlasting covenant" (13:20). By the eternal Spirit the blood has obtained an eternal, ever-availing, ever-fresh, independent, imperishable power of life.

The Spirit manifests His full power and works effectively among men only through the blood. As the blood possesses its power through the Spirit, the correlative is also true. We know that the outpouring of the blood was followed by the outpouring of the Spirit. And we know the reason for this: because of sin, a middle wall of partition separated God and man. "The flesh" was the veil that made true union impossible. As long as sin was not atoned for, God by His Spirit could not take up a settled abode in the heart of man. Until the power of the flesh was broken and subdued, the Spirit could not manifest His authority. For this reason there is no mention in the days of the Old Testament of an outpouring of the Spirit of God, except as a prediction of what would be in the last days. Therefore, also, our Lord Jesus was not in a position to bestow upon His disciples the Spirit with whom He had been baptized, even though He took them into the closest fellowship with Himself, and though He greatly loved them and longed to bless them.

Our Lord had to die before He could baptize with the Holy Spirit. The blood is the life of man; the Spirit is the life of God. Man must sacrifice his sinful life, bear the penalty of his sin, and surrender himself entirely to God before God can dwell in him with His life. What man himself could not do, that the Lord

Jesus, the Son of Man, did for him. He shed His blood; He gave His life in entire surrender to the will of God as a satisfaction— a payment of the penalty for sin. When that was accomplished, it was possible for Him to receive the Spirit from the Father, that He might pour Him out. The outpouring of the blood rendered possible the outpouring of the Spirit.

This is declared in Scripture in such words as these: "The Holy Spirit was not yet given, because Jesus was not yet glorified" (John 7:39). And again: "He showed me a pure river of water of life, clear as crystal, proceeding from the throne of God and of the Lamb" (Rev. 22:1). It was when the Lamb took possession of the throne with the Father that the Spirit could flow out as a river. Hence, in the preaching of John the Baptist these were the two statements he made about Jesus: "Behold! The Lamb of God who takes away the sin of the world!" and "This is He who baptizes with the Holy Spirit."

It was necessary for our High Priest to enter into "the Holiest"* with His blood, and, having come out again, to appear before the Father's throne with that blood, before He could bestow the Spirit from the throne as the seal that His work in the Holiest had accomplished a perfect reconciliation. The blood and the Spirit are inseparable, for only through the blood can the Spirit dwell in man.

The activities of the blood and the Spirit are inseparably connected in the execution of the work of redemption. This is why we find in Scripture that what in one place is ascribed to the Spirit is in another place ascribed to the blood, and the work of sanctification is ascribed to both the blood and the Spirit. Life also is ascribed to both. Our Lord said: "Whoever eats My flesh and drinks

* Derived from Hebrews 10:19. It is called "the Holiest of All" in Hebrews 9:3 and 8. The earthly equivalent was more commonly referred to as "the Most Holy Place" (Exodus 26:33–34) or—see many modern translations— "the Holy of Holies."

My blood has eternal life," adding afterwards, "It is the Spirit who gives life; the flesh profits nothing" (John 6:54, 63). We find similar expressions in the Epistle to the Ephesians. After having said "You . . . have been made near by the blood of Christ" (2:13), a little later Paul declares (verse 18) that "We . . . have access by one Spirit to the Father." So also in the Epistle to the Hebrews: the scorning of the blood and of the Spirit are treated as one act. We read there of those "who counted the blood of the covenant by which he was sanctified a common thing, and in-sulted the Spirit of grace" (Heb. 10:29).

We have noticed that "the blood" is a phrase chosen by God as a short way of expressing certain thoughts, powers, and dispo-sitions, which are, as it were, included in it. It is not always easy, either in preaching or in personal exercise of faith, to find a per-fect expression of these thoughts, powers, and dispositions. But this is what the Holy Spirit undertakes as His work, especially where faith is exercised about the blood; He will explain, and make living, the full and glorious meaning of the word. By en-lightening our understanding, He will make clear to us the great thoughts of God which are contained in the words "the blood." Even before the understanding can lay hold of them, He will make their power active in the soul; and where a heart which is desiring salvation is humbly and reverently seeking for the bless-ings they bring, He will bestow them. He will not only send the power of the blood *to* the heart, but will so reveal it *in* the heart that the same disposition which inspired Jesus in the shedding of His blood will be awakened in us, as it is written: "And they overcame him by the blood of the Lamb, . . . and they did not love their lives to the death" (Rev. 12:11).

It is the great work of the Holy Spirit to glorify Jesus—to make Him glorious in human hearts by bestowing the blessed experience of His redemption. And because the blood is the cen-tral point of redemption, the Holy Spirit will not only make the blood appear uniquely glorious *to* us but will glorify it *in* us. We can form some idea of the blood that was shed on earth in connection with the sin offering, but we have little conception of the blood that in "the Holiest" on high speaks and works in the power of eternal life. The Holy Spirit, however, comes with His heavenly, life-giving power to enable us to appropriate that which is eternal, and to make it a real, living, inward experience within us.

The atoning efficacy of the blood and the personality of the Holy Spirit are two truths which are both denied when the church turns aside to error, while both of them are held fast in faith by the true Church of God. Where the blood is honored, preached, and believed in as the power of full redemption, there the way is opened for the fullness of the Spirit's blessing. And in proportion as the Holy Spirit truly works in the hearts of men, He always leads them to glory in the blood of the Lamb. "And I looked, and behold, in the midst of the throne . . . stood a Lamb as though it had been slain, having . . . seven horns and seven eyes, which are the seven Spirits of God" (Rev. 5:6). The blood and the Spirit proceed together from the Lamb, and together they bear witness to Him alone.

II. The Union of the Blood and the Spirit in Our Personal Experience.

We lay emphasis on this to show what rich comfort and blessing this truth contains for us. We must once again notice the two sides of this truth: the blood exercises its full efficacy through the Spirit, and the Spirit manifests His full power through the blood.

The blood exercises its full power through the Spirit. We have here a glorious answer to the questions that at once arise in the minds of seekers after salvation. I have no doubt that because of what has been written on the power of the blood of Jesus—about the rich, full blessing which is found in that blood—many questions have arisen, such as:

"How is it that the blood is not more efficacious in my life?"

"How can I experience its full power?"

"Is there any hope for a person as weak as I am, and one who understands so little, to expect that fullness of blessing?"

Listen to the answer, all you who heartily and sincerely long for it. The Holy Spirit dwells within you, and it is His office to glorify the Lamb and the blood of the Lamb. The Spirit and the blood bear witness together. The mistake we make is in thinking of the blood as if it alone bears witness. We think of the shedding of the blood as an event that occurred nineteen hundred years ago, on which we are to look back, and by the exercise of faith to represent it as present and real—and, as our faith is always weak, we feel that we cannot do this as it ought to be done. As a result of this mistaken idea, we have no powerful experience of what the blood can do.

This weakness of faith arises, in the case of honest hearts, from imperfect conceptions concerning the power of the blood. If I regard the blood not as something which lies inactive and which must be aroused to activity by my faith, but, rather, as an almighty, eternal power which is always active, then my faith becomes for the first time a true faith. Then I shall understand that my weakness cannot interfere with the power of the blood. I have simply to honor the blood by worthy, right-minded ideas of its power to overcome every hindrance. The blood *will* manifest its power in me, because the eternal Spirit of God always works *with* it and *in* it.

Was it not through the eternal Spirit that, when Jesus died, His blood had power to conquer sin and death, so that Jesus was "brought up . . . from the dead . . . through the blood of the everlasting covenant" (Heb. 13:20)?

Was it not through the eternal Spirit that the blood penetrated the regions of holy light and life to heaven itself and bears there its peculiar relationship to God the Father, and to Jesus the Mediator?

Is it not through the eternal Spirit that the blood ever continues to manifest its power on the innumerable multitude which is being gathered together?

Is it not the eternal Spirit who dwells in me as a child of God, and on whom also I may rely to make the blood of Jesus glorious in me? Thank God, it is so. I have no need to fear. In a childlike heart, conscious of its weakness and wholly surrendered to the Lamb of God in order to experience the power of His blood, the Holy Spirit will do His work. We may confidently rely upon the Spirit to reveal in us the omnipotent effects of the blood.

But there is another difficulty. When we recognize that the blood is omnipotent in its effects, then we so often limit the continuance of its activities to the period of our own active cooperation with it. You imagine that, so long as you *think* about it, and your faith is actively engaged with it, the blood will manifest its power in you. But there is a very large part of your life during which you must be engaged with earthly business, and you do not believe that during these hours the blood can continue its active work quite undisturbed. And yet it is so. If you have the necessary faith, if you definitely commit yourself to the sanctifying power of the blood for those hours during which you cannot be thinking about it, then you can be sure that your soul will continue, undisturbed, under the blessed activities of the blood. That is the meaning, the comfort, of what we said about the word "eternal," and the "eternal redemption" which the blood has purchased. Eternal is that in which "the power of an imperishable life" works ceaselessly every moment. Through the eternal Spirit, the precious blood possesses this ceaselessly efficacious power of eternal life. So the soul may, with even greater confidence, entrust itself to Him for every hour of business engagements, or of special rush and bustle; for the activity of the blood will continue without hindrance. Just as a fountain which is supplied by or from an abundant store of water streams out day and night with a cleansing and refreshing flow, so the blessed streams of this fountain of life will flow over and through the soul that dares to expect it from his or her Lord.

And just as the Holy Spirit is the life-power of these omnipotent and ever-flowing streams of the blessed efficacy of the blood, so it is He also who prepares us and makes it possible for us to recognize and receive these streams by faith.

Spiritual things must be spiritually discerned. Our human thought cannot comprehend the mysteries of "the Holiest" in heaven. This is especially true concerning the unspeakable glory of the holy blood in heaven. Let us with deep reverence entrust ourselves to the teaching of the Spirit, waiting on Him in holy stillness and awe that He may witness with, and about, the blood.

As often as we longingly pray for the holy power of the blood, let us with great tenderness open our hearts to the influences of the Spirit; for the Spirit and the blood always bear witness together. Through the eternal Spirit the full power of the blood will be exercised in us.

There is another glorious side to this truth:

The Spirit attains His full power in us through the blood. Just as the outpouring of the Spirit followed the outpouring of the blood and its translation into heaven, so is it also in the heart. In proportion as the blood obtains a place in the heart, and is honored there, so the Spirit is free to carry on His work.

On Ascension Day we remember the passion and resurrection of our Lord, and look forward to Pentecost** and the days of prayer during which we wait on the Lord that we may be filled

---

** Note by the Translator: The Dutch Reformed Church in South Africa for many years observed the ten days between Ascension and Pentecost as days

by His Spirit. We are thus reminded that it is the will of Him "who baptizes with the Holy Spirit" that His disciples should be filled with the Spirit. "Full of the Holy Spirit" is not set forth in Scripture as the privilege of a particular time, or of a certain people, but is plainly represented as the privilege of every believer who surrenders himself to live wholly for, and in fellowship with, Jesus. Pentecost is not just a remembrance of something that once happened and then passed away, but it is the celebration of the opening of a fountain which ever flows, and it is the promise of that which is always the right, and the characteristic, of those who belong to the Lord. We ought to be, and we must be, filled with the Holy Spirit.

The lesson which the Word of God has taught us shows the preparation necessary for the baptism of the Spirit. For the first disciples, as well as for the Lord Jesus, the path to Pentecost ran by Golgotha. The outpouring of the Spirit is inseparably bound up with the previous outpouring of the blood. With us also it is a new and deeper experience of what the blood can accomplish that will lead us to the full blessing of Pentecost.

If you long for this blessing, consider, I beseech you, the immovable foundation on which it rests. Take such a word as that from John: "The blood of Jesus Christ His Son cleanses us from all sin" (1 John 1:7). The *cleansed* vessel can be *filled.* Come with all the sins of which you are conscious, and ask the Lamb to cleanse you in His blood. Receive that word with a perfect faith, with a faith that rejoices beyond all feeling and experience—"It has taken place for *me.*" Faith acts as possessing what it does not feel; it knows how to now take and possess in the spirit that which only later on will be realized in the soul and in the body.

Walking in the light, you have a right to say with perfect liberty, "The blood of Jesus Christ cleanses *me* from all sin." Rely

---

of continuous and united prayer. It is impossible to tell how great and abiding has been the blessing of God on these gatherings.

on your Great High Priest to manifest in your heart also, by His Spirit, the heavenly wonder-working power which His blood has exercised for cleansing in "the Holiest." Rely on the blood of the Lamb which destroyed the authority and effect of sin before God, in heaven, to destroy it also in your heart. And let your song of joy, by faith, be "Unto Him who cleansed *me* in His own blood be glory and dominion," and reckon on receiving the fullness of the Spirit. It is by the Spirit that the blood was offered up. It is by the Spirit that the blood has had its power in your heart, and is still efficacious there. It is by the Spirit that your heart, through the blood, has been made a temple of God. Reckon, with full assurance of faith, that a heart which is, through Him, "by blood made clean" is prepared as a temple to be filled with the glory of God. Reckon on the fullness of the Spirit as *your* portion.

Oh, the blessedness of a heart "by blood made clean," and filled with the Spirit; full of joy and full of love, full of faith and full of praise, full of zeal and full of power—for the work of the Lord. By the blood and the Spirit of the Lamb, that heart is a temple where God dwells on His throne of grace, where God Himself is the light, where God's will is the only law, where the glory of God is all in all. Oh, ye children of God, come and let the precious blood prepare you for being filled with His Spirit, so that the Lamb that was slain for you may have the reward of His labor—labor marked by blood—and He and you together may be satisfied in His love.

4

The Blood of the Cross

"For it pleased the Father . . . to reconcile all things to Himself, by Him, whether things on earth or things in heaven, having made peace through the blood of His cross."—Colossians 1:19–20.

THE Apostle Paul uses here an expression of deep significance: "the blood of His cross." We know how greatly he valued the expression "the cross of Christ." It expressed, in a brief phrase, the entire power and blessing of the death of our Lord for our redemption. It was the key subject of Paul's preaching, the hope and glory of his life. By the expression here used he shows how, on the one side, the blood receives its value from the cross on which it was shed; and on the other, that it is through the blood that the cross reveals its effect and power. Thus the cross and the blood throw reflected light on one another. In our inquiry concerning the power of the blood, we shall find it of great importance to consider what this expression has to teach us—what is meant by the blood as "the blood of the cross." It will enable us to view from a new standpoint the truths which we have already discovered in that phrase "the blood."

Let us fix our attention on the following points:

    I.   The disposition of our Lord from which the cross derived its value.

   II.   The power which the cross has thus obtained.

  III.   The love which the cross reveals.

I. The Disposition of Our Lord from Which the Cross Derived Its Value.

We are so accustomed, in speaking about the cross of Christ, to think only of the work that was done there for us that we take too little notice of what that work derives its value from—the inner disposition of our Lord, of which the cross was only the outward expression. Scripture does not place in the foreground, as most important, the weighty and bitter sufferings of the Lord, which are often emphasized for the purpose of awakening religious feelings, but rather the inner disposition of the Lord which led Him to the cross, and inspired Him while on it—this Scripture does emphasize. Neither does Scripture direct attention only to the work which the Lord accomplished *for us* on the cross; it clearly directs special attention to the work that the cross accomplished in Christ and which through Him must yet be accomplished *in us*.

This appears not only from our Lord's words which He spoke from the cross, but from what He said when on three different occasions He had previously told His disciples that they must take up their cross and follow Him. More than once He spoke thus when foretelling His own crucifixion. The thought He wished particularly to impress upon them in connection with the cross was that of fellowship with and of conformity to Him. That this did not consist in merely outward sufferings and persecutions, but in an inward disposition, appears from what He often added: "Deny yourselves and take up the cross." This is what He desires them to do. Our Lord further teaches us that neither for Him nor for His disciples does the bearing of the cross begin when a material cross is laid upon the shoulders. No! He carried the cross all through His life; what became visible on Golgotha was a manifestation of the disposition which inspired His whole life.

What then did the bearing of the cross mean for the Lord

Jesus? And what end could it serve for Him? We know that the evil of sin appears in the change it brought about both in the disposition of man towards God and in that of God towards man. With man it resulted in his fall from God, or enmity against God; with God it resulted in His turning away from man, or His wrath. In the first we see the terribleness of sin's tyranny over man; in the second, the terribleness of the guilt of sin, demanding the judgment of God on man.

The Lord Jesus, who came to deliver man from sin as a whole, had to deal with the power of sin as well as with its guilt. First the one, and then the other. For although we separate these two things for the sake of making truth clear, sin is ever a unity. Therefore we need to understand not only that our Lord by His atonement on the cross removed the *guilt* of sin, but that this was made possible by the victory He had first won over the *power* of sin. It is the glory of the cross that it was the divine means by which both these objects were accomplished.

The Lord Jesus had to bring to naught the power of sin. He could do this only in His own person. Therefore He came in the closest possible likeness of sinful flesh—in the weakness of flesh, with the fullest capacity to be tempted as we are. From His baptism with the Holy Spirit and the temptation of Satan which followed, up to the fearful soul agony in Gethsemane and the offering of Himself on the cross, His life was a ceaseless strife against self-will and self-honor—against the temptations of the flesh and of the world to, by those means, reach His goal: the setting up of His kingdom. Every day He had to take up and carry His cross—that is, to lose His own life and will—by going out of Himself and doing and speaking nothing but what He had seen or heard from the Father. That which took place in the temptation in the wilderness and in the agony of Gethsemane—at the beginning and the end of His public ministry—is only a peculiarly clear manifestation of the disposition which characterized His whole life. He was recurrently tempted to the sin of self-assertion—from the first temptation, to obtain bread to satisfy His hunger, till the last, that He might not have to drink the bitter cup of death—but He overcame these temptations to satisfy lawful desires and chose, rather, to be subject to the will of the Father.

So He offered up Himself and His life; He denied Himself, and took up His cross; He learned obedience and was perfected (Heb. 5:9). In His own person He gained a complete victory over the power of sin, till He was able to testify concerning the evil one, "The ruler of this world is coming, and he has nothing in Me."

His death on the cross was the last and most glorious achievement in His personal victory over the power of sin. From this the atoning death of the cross derived its value, for a reconciliation was necessary if guilt was to be removed. No one can contend with sin without at the same time coming into conflict with the wrath of God. These two cannot be separated from one another. The Lord Jesus desired to deliver man from his sin. He could not do this except by suffering death as Mediator, and in that death suffering the curse of God's wrath against sin, and bearing it away. But His supreme power to remove guilt and the curse did not lie merely in the fact that He endured so much pain and suffering at death, but that He endured it all *in willing obedience to the Father*, for the maintenance and glorification of His Father's righteousness. It was this disposition of self-sacrifice, of bearing the cross willingly, which bestowed on the cross its power.

So the Scripture says: "He became obedient to the point of death, even the death of the cross. Therefore God also has highly exalted Him and given Him the name which is above every name" (Phil. 2:8–9).

And again: "Yet He learned obedience by the things which He suffered. And having been perfected, He became the author of eternal salvation to all who obey Him" (Heb. 5:8–9). It is because Jesus broke down and conquered the power of sin first in His personal life that He can remove from us the guilt of sin, and thus deliver us from both its power and guilt. The cross is the divine sign, proclaiming to us that the way—the only way to the life of God—is through the yielding up in sacrifice of the self-life.

Now this spirit of obedience, this sacrifice of self which bestowed on the cross its infinite value, bestowed that value also on the *blood* of the cross. Here again God reveals to us the secret of the power of that blood. That blood is the proof of obedience unto death by the beloved Son; proof of that disposition in which He chose to shed His blood and lose His life rather than commit the sin of pleasing Himself; proof of the sacrifice of everything, even life itself, to glorify the Father. The life which dwelt in that blood—the heart from which it flowed, glowing with love and devotion to God and His will—was one of entire obedience and consecration to Him.

And now what do you think? If that blood, living and powerful through the Holy Spirit, comes into contact with our hearts, and if we rightly understand what the blood of the cross means, is it possible that that blood should not impart its holy nature to us? But as the blood could not have been shed apart from the sacrifice of "self" on the cross, so it cannot be received or enjoyed apart from a similar sacrifice of "self." That blood will bring to us a self-sacrificing disposition, and in our work there will be a conformity to, and an imitation of, the crucified One, making self-sacrifice the highest and most blessed law of our lives. The blood is a living, spiritual, heavenly power. It will bring the soul that is entirely surrendered to it to see and know by experience that there is no entrance into the full life of God but by the self-sacrifice of the cross.

II. The Power Which the Cross Has Obtained by This Disposition.

As we pay attention to this we shall have a deeper insight into the meaning of the cross and "the blood of the cross." The Apostle Paul speaks of the message of the cross as "the power of God."

We want to know what the cross as the power of God can accomplish. We have seen the twofold relationship our Lord had towards sin. First, He needed in Himself, as man, to subdue its *power*; then He could destroy its effects before God, such as *guilt*. The one was a process carried on throughout His human life; the other took place in the hour of His passion. Now that He has completed His work, we may receive both blessings at the same time. Sin is a unity; so is redemption. We receive, in an equal share, both deliverance from the power of sin and acquittal from its guilt—and at the same time. As far as consciousness is concerned, however, acquittal from guilt comes earlier than a clear sense of the forgiveness of sins. It cannot be otherwise. Our Lord Jesus had first to obtain the blotting out of guilt through His victory over sin, and then He arose and ascended to heaven. The blessing comes to us in the reverse order: redemption descends upon us as a gift from above, and therefore restoration of a right relationship to God comes first—deliverance from guilt. Along with that, and flowing from it, comes deliverance from the power of sin.

This twofold deliverance we owe to the power of the cross. Paul speaks of the first, deliverance from guilt, in the words of our text. He says that God has become reconciled, "having made peace through the blood of His cross" with a view to reconciling all things to Himself.

Sin had brought about a change in God; not in His nature, but in His relationship towards us. He had to turn away from us in wrath. Peace has been made through the cross of Christ. By reconciliation for sin, God has reconciled us with and united us to Himself.

The power of the cross in heaven has been manifested in the entire removal of everything that could bring about a separation from God, or awaken His wrath, so that in Christ we are granted the utmost freedom of intimate entrance into His presence. Peace has been made, and proclaimed. This peace reigns in heaven, for we are perfectly reconciled to God, and have been received again into His friendship.

All this is through the power of the cross. Oh, that we had eyes to see how completely the veil has been rent, how free and unhindered is our access to God, and how freely His blessing may flow towards us! There is now nothing, absolutely nothing, to hinder the fullness of the love and power of God from coming to us and working in us—except our unbelief, our slowness of heart. Let us meditate upon the power which the blood has exercised in heaven until our unbelief itself is conquered and our right to these heavenly powers by faith fills our lives with joy!

But the powerful effect of the cross with God in heaven, in the blotting out of guilt and bringing about our renewed union with Him, is, as we have seen, inseparable from that other effect—the breaking down of the authority of sin over man by the sacrifice of "self." Therefore Scripture teaches us that the cross not only works out a disposition or desire to make such a sacrifice, but it really bestows the power to do so, and completes the work. This appears with wonderful clearness in the Epistle to the Galatians. In one place the cross is spoken of as the reconciliation for guilt. "Christ has redeemed us from the curse of the law, having become a curse for us (for it is written, 'Cursed is everyone who hangs on a tree')" (Gal. 3:13).

But there are three other places where the cross is even more plainly spoken of as the victory over the power of sin—as the power to put to death the "I" of the self-life, of the flesh, and of the world. "I have been crucified with Christ; it is no longer I who live, but Christ lives in me" (Gal. 2:20). "And those who are Christ's have crucified the flesh with its passions and desires" (Gal. 5:24). "But God forbid that I should glory except in the cross of our Lord Jesus Christ, by whom the world has been crucified to me, and I to the world" (Gal. 6:14). In these passages our union with Christ, the crucified One, and the conformity to Him resulting from that union, are represented as the result of the power exercised on us by the cross.

To understand this we must remember that when Jesus chose the cross, and took it up, and carried it, and finally died on it, He did this as the Second Adam, as the Head and Surety of His people. What He did, had and retains power for them, and exercises that power in those who understand and believe this. The life which He bestows on them is a life in which the cross is the most outstanding characteristic. Our Lord carried His cross all through His entire life as Mediator. By dying on that cross as Mediator, He obtained the life of glory. As the believer is united to Him and receives His life, he receives a life that, through the cross, has overthrown the power of sin, and he can henceforth say, "I have been crucified with Christ." "I know that my old man was crucified with Christ"; "I am dead to sin"; "I have crucified the flesh"; "I have been crucified to the world" (Rom. 6:6, 11; Gal. 6:14).

All these expressions from God's Word refer to something that occurred in a time now past. The life and attitude of Jesus bestows on believers their share in the victory over sin which was achieved on the cross. And now in the power of this participation and fellowship, they live as Jesus lived; they live always as those crucified to themselves—as those who know that their "old man" and "flesh" are crucified so as to be put to death. In the power of this fellowship they live as Jesus lived. They have the power in all things and at all times to choose the cross in spite of the "old man" and the world—to choose the cross and to let it do its work.

The law of life for Jesus was the surrender of His own will to that of the Father, by giving up that life to death so as to enter upon the heavenly life of redemption—by the cross, to the throne. Just as surely as there is a kingdom of sin, under the authority of which we were brought by our connection with the first Adam, so surely has there been set up a new kingdom of grace, in Christ Jesus, under the powerful influence of which we are brought by faith. The marvelous power by which Jesus subdued sin on the cross lives and works in us, and not only calls us to life as He lived, but *enables* us to do so—to adopt the cross as the motto and law of our lives.

Believer, that blood with which you have been sprinkled, under which you live daily, is the blood of the cross. It obtains its power from the fact that it was the complete sacrifice of a life to God. The blood and the cross are inseparably united. The blood *comes* from the cross; it *bears witness* to the cross; it *leads* to the cross. The power of the cross is in that blood. And every touch of the blood should inspire you with a fresh ability to take the cross as the law of your life. "Not my will, but Yours be done" may, now, in that power, become a song of daily consecration. What the cross teaches you, that it bestows upon you; what it imposes upon you, that it makes possible for you. Let the everlasting sprinkling of the blood of the cross be your choice, and through that blood the disposition as well as the power of the cross will be seen in you.

III. The Love Which the Cross Reveals.

We must now fix our attention on this, if we are to learn the full glory of the blood of the cross.

We have spoken of the disposition of which the cross is the expression, and of the powerful influence that disposition exercises in us and through us if we allow the blood of the cross to have its full power over us. The fear, however, often arises in the mind of the Christian that it is too much of a burden always to preserve and manifest that attitude of crucifixion; and even the assurance that the cross is "the power of God" which produces this disposition does not entirely remove that fear, since the exercise of that power depends to some extent on our surrender and faith, and these are far from being what they ought to be. Can we find in the cross a deliverance from this infirmity, the healing of this disease? Cannot "the blood of the cross" make us partakers always, without ceasing, not only of the blotting out of guilt but also of victory over the power of sin?

It can. Draw near, to hear once more what the cross proclaims to you. It is only when we understand aright, and receive into our hearts the love of which the cross speaks, that we can experience its full power and blessing. Paul indeed bears witness to this: "I have been crucified with Christ; it is no longer I who live, but Christ lives in me; and the life which I now live in the flesh I live by faith in the Son of God, who loved me and gave Himself for me" (Gal. 2:20).

Faith in the love of Him "who gave Himself for me" on the cross enables me to live as one who has been crucified with Him.

The cross is the revelation of love. Christ saw that there was no way by which His love could redeem those whom He so loved except by His shedding His blood for them on the cross. It is because of this that He would not allow Himself to be turned aside by the terror of the cross, not even when it caused His soul to tremble and shudder. The cross tells us that He loved us so truly that His love surmounted every difficulty—the curse of sin, and the hostility of man—and that His love has conquered and has won us for Himself. The cross is the triumphant symbol of eternal love. By the cross, love is seated on the throne, so that from the place of omnipotence it can now do for the beloved ones all that they desire.

What a new and glorious light is thus shed on the demand

the cross makes on me, and on what it offers to do for me; on the meaning, and glory, and life of the cross, to which I have been called by the Word—I, whose flesh is so disposed to go astray that even the promise of the Spirit and the power of heaven seem insufficient to bestow on me the courage I need. But lo, here is something that is better still than the promise of power! The cross points out to me the living Jesus in His eternal, all-conquering love. Out of love to us He gave Himself up to the cross, to redeem a people for Himself. In this love He accepts everyone who comes to Him in the fellowship of His cross, to bestow upon them all the blessings that He has obtained on that cross. And now He receives us into the power of His eternal and ever-efficacious love, which ceases not for one moment to work out in us what He obtained for us on the cross.

I see it! What we need is a right view of Jesus Himself, and of His all-conquering, eternal love. The blood is the earthly token of the heavenly glory of that love; the blood points to that love. What we need is to behold Jesus Himself in the light of the cross. All the love manifested by the cross is the measure of the love He bears to us today. The love which was not terrified by any power or opposition of sin will now conquer everything in us that would be a hindrance. The love which triumphed on the accursed tree is strong enough to obtain and maintain a complete victory over us. The love manifested by "a Lamb looking as if it had been slain" who is now the throne, bearing always the marks of the cross, lives solely to bestow on us the disposition, and power, and the blessing of the cross. To know Jesus in His love, and to live in that love—to have the heart filled with that love—is the greatest blessing that the cross can bring to us. It is the way to the enjoyment of all the blessings of the cross.

Glorious cross! Glorious cross, which brings to us and makes known to us the eternal love. The blood is the fruit and power of the cross; the blood is the gift and bestowal of that love. In what a full enjoyment of love those may now live who have been brought into such wonderful contact with the blood, who live every moment under its cleansing. How wondrously that blood unites us to Jesus and His love. He is the High Priest, out of whose heart that blood streamed and to whose heart that blood returns, the one who is Himself the reason for the sprinkling of the blood—who Himself perfects the sprinkling of the blood in order that by it He may take possession of the heart that He on the cross has won. He is the High Priest who in the tenderness of love now lives to perfect everything in us, so that the disposition which the cross has established as the *law* of our lives, and the victory which the cross offers us as the *power* of our lives, may be realized by us.

Beloved Christian, whose hope is in the blood of the cross, give yourself up to experience its full blessing. Each drop of that blood points to the surrender and death of self-will—the "I" life—as the way to God and victorious life in Him. Each drop of that blood assures you of the power of a life, a heavenly life, obtained by Jesus on the cross, to maintain that disposition, that crucified life, in you. Each drop of that blood brings to you Jesus and His eternal love, to work out all the blessing of the cross in you and to keep you in that love.

May each thought of the cross and the blood bring you nearer to your Savior—yes, into a deeper union with Him to whom they point you. Amen.

5

The Altar Sanctified by the Blood

A Communion Message

"Seven days you shall make atonement for the altar and sanctify it. And the altar shall be most holy. Whatever touches the altar must be holy"— Exodus 29:37.

OF ALL the articles in the furnishing of the tabernacle, the altar of brass was in many respects the most important. The golden mercy seat over which God manifested His visible glory in the "most holy place," behind the veil, was definitely more glorious; it was, however, hidden from the eyes of Israel, being the representation of the hidden presence of God in heaven. Only once in the year was Israel's active faith intentionally fixed on it. But at the brazen altar, on the other hand, every day God's priests were continually engaged. This altar might be likened to a door of entrance to all the service of God, being in the "holy place" of the tabernacle.

Before there was either a temple or a tabernacle, an altar served as a place for the worship of God—as in the case of Noah and the other patriarchs. Man may worship God without a temple if he has an altar, but he may not worship God without an altar—even if he has a temple. Before God spoke to Moses at Sinai about a tabernacle where He might dwell among the people, He had already spoken to him about sacrificial worship. The service of the altar was the beginning, the center, indeed the heart of the service of the tabernacle and temple.

Why was that? What was the altar? And why did it occupy such an important position? The Hebrew word for "altar" gives the answer. It means, specifically, "the place of putting to death, as a sacrifice." Even the altar of incense—the golden altar, where no slain victim was offered—bore the name of altar, because the incense burning on it was an offering to the Lord. The chief thought is this: that man's service for God consists in the sacrifice and consecration of himself and all he has to God. To this end there had to be a separated place, ordered and sanctified by God Himself. Because the altar has been ordered and sanctified by Him, it sanctifies and makes the gift that is laid upon it acceptable. The offerer brings to it not only the sacrifice that is to atone for his sins, but also the thank offering that follows reconciliation (2 Chron. 29:31)—as the expression of his love and thankfulness, including his desire for closer fellowship with God and the full enjoyment of His favor. The altar is the place of sacrifice, of consecration, and also of fellowship with God.

The brazen altar of the Old Testament must have an antitype in the New Testament—something that in spiritual worship is the perfect reality of which the Old Testament altar was only the shadow. "We have an altar," declares the inspired writer in Hebrews 13:10. That altar in the New Testament, no less than that of the Old Testament, was a place for putting to death—a place of sacrifice. It is the altar where, "once for all," the Lamb of God was sacrificed as the great sin offering, where also each believer must present himself with all that he has as a thank offering to God. That "altar" is the cross.

In our text we learn that the brazen altar itself initially had to be sanctified by blood if it was to possess the power of sanctifying whatever touched it.

Our text tells us about:

I. The altar that was sanctified by blood.

II. The offerings that are sanctified by the altar.

May the Spirit of God open our eyes to see the full power of the blood of the cross, particularly in the sanctification of the cross as the place of our death, where we also may be consecrated to God.

I. The Altar That Was Sanctified by Blood.

It is in the midst of the instructions concerning the consecration of Aaron as High Priest (his sons being consecrated with him as priests) that the words of the text appear. A priest must have an altar. But just as the priest himself had to be sanctified by blood, so was it also with the altar. God commanded that a sin offering should be prepared to cleanse the altar and to make atonement for it.

For seven days Moses had to carry on this work of making atonement for the altar.

We read: "And Moses killed [the sin offering]. Then he took the blood, and put some on the horns of the altar all around with his finger, and purified the altar; and he poured the blood at the base of the altar, and sanctified it, to make atonement for it" (Lev. 8:15). By this "atonement," not only was the altar sanctified and made "holy," but it was made "most holy"—"a holy of holies." This expression is the same as that used to describe the inner shrine of the tabernacle where God dwelt. It is used here of the altar, which had a similar, special measure of holiness. The one was the hidden, the other the approachable "holy of holies." Then we read: "Whatever touches the altar must ['shall,' A.V.] be holy" (Exod. 29:37). By the sevenfold atoning with blood the altar had obtained such a holiness that it had the power of sanctifying everything that was laid upon it. The Israelite had no need to fear that his offering might be too small or too unworthy; the altar sanctified the gift that was laid upon it. Our Lord referred to this as a well-known fact when He asked, "For which is greater, the gift or the altar that sanctifies the gift?" (Matt. 23:19). The altar, by the sevenfold sprinkling of the blood, sanctified every offering which was laid upon it.

What a glorious fresh light this word sheds on "the power of the blood of Jesus," and on His cross, which is sanctified by His blood. We have already inquired how it is that the blood obtained its value from the cross. As blood—proof of the surrender of the life of Christ in obedience unto death—it has power to make reconciliation and to obtain victory over sin. But lo!—here a fresh glory of the blood is revealed to us. The cross on which it was shed is not only the altar on which Jesus was sacrificed, but it has been consecrated by that blood as an altar on which we also may be sacrificed and made acceptable to God.

It is the cross alone, as sanctified by blood—yes, sanctified to be a "holy of holies," which sanctifies everything that touches it—that has this power.

In heathen worship, and also in Romanism, people are often taught a doctrine about a cross: that by self-imposed suffering and self-sacrifice, they may become pleasing to God. But they seek a value in the sufferings themselves, as a putting to death of the flesh. They do not understand that everything that man does, whether it be suffering or sacrifice, is stained by sin, and is thus incapable of really conquering sin, or pleasing God. They do not understand that even the cross itself, as the means of self-sacrifice, must first be sanctified. Before the sufferings of a cross can sanctify us, it must itself first be sanctified.

For this purpose God made a most glorious provision. He caused an "altar" to be erected for which a sevenfold and thus a perfect reconciliation had been made, so that whatever touched that altar was holy. By the blood of the Son of God the cross has become "most holy": a "holy of holies," with power to sanctify us.

We know how this has been accomplished. We cannot too often speak or think about it, nor believe it and be thankful enough for it. By shedding His precious, divine blood as a sacrifice for our sin, after surrendering Himself in perfect obedience to the will of the Father and having personal victory over sin—by bearing our punishment and curse, Jesus has conquered sin and rendered it powerless for us also.

What Jesus did and suffered on the cross, He did and suffered as the Second Adam, as our Surety, our Head. He showed us there that the only way to be freed from the flesh—in the likeness and weakness of which He came—so as to enter into the life of God and of the Spirit, was by surrendering the flesh to the righteous judgment of God. The only way into the life of God was through the death of the flesh.

But not merely did He show us that this was the only way, but by His death He obtained the right and power to enable us to walk in that very way. Our natural life is so entirely under the authority of sin that we cannot be delivered from it by any sufferings or sacrifices or endeavors of our own. But the life and sufferings of Jesus have such a divine power that by them the authority of sin has been entirely destroyed, and everyone who seeks the way to God, and to the *life* of God through sacrifice and death in fellowship with Him, will find that way and be enabled to walk in it.

Through the blood of Jesus—through the perfect reconciliation and the power of an eternal life which His blood has revealed—the cross of Jesus has been sanctified forever as an altar on which alone everything that is presented to God must be offered.

The cross is an altar. We have seen that an altar is a place for slaying, a place of sacrifice. The place where the incense was offered was also called an altar. On both the altar of sacrifice and the altar of incense, a fire burned. What is presented to God must first pass through death and then be consumed by fire. In its natural condition it is unclean, and judgment must be executed upon it; any gift must be consumed by fire, and in a new, spiritual form borne heavenwards.

What the altar of sacrifice—the cross—proclaims about Christ is the law in the temple of a holy God: there is no way to God except through death, through the sacrifice of life. There is no way to God nor to heaven for us save by the cross.

And the cross is not merely that physical cross on which we are to believe that Jesus died for our sins. No, but there is the cross on which we must die. The Lord Jesus early and repeatedly warned His disciples that He must be crucified, and that they must each bear their cross after Him; each one must be prepared to be crucified even as He was. By that He did not mean merely outward suffering or death; no, He spoke of the inner self-denial, of the hating and losing the self-life, as being the fellowship of His cross. This was before His crucifixion. The Holy Spirit teaches us by the Apostle Paul how we are to speak about the cross after Jesus had been put to death on it: "I have been crucified with Christ"; "Those who are Christ's have crucified the flesh with its passions and desires"; "God forbid that I should glory except in the cross of our Lord Jesus Christ, by whom the world has been crucified to me, and I to the world." These three passages in the Epistle to the Galatians teach us that we are not to regard the sufferings on the cross as being only the expiation of our guilt, but as the characteristic and the power of our lives. In the cross the life of Jesus on earth attained its purpose, its climax, its perfection; apart from the cross He could not have been the Christ. The life of Christ from heaven bears the same characteristic in us: it is the life of the crucified One. The phrase "I have been crucified with Christ" is inseparable from the one which follows: "Christ lives in me." Each day and each hour we must abide in the place of crucifixion; each moment the power of the cross of

Christ must work in us—we must be made conformable unto His death. Then the power of God will be manifested in us. The weakness and death of the cross is ever coupled with the life and power of God. Paul says: "For though He [Christ] was crucified in weakness, yet He lives by the power of God. For we also are weak in Him, but we shall live with Him by the power of God toward you" (2 Cor. 13:4).

Many Christians do not understand this. The cross in which they glory differs from that in which Paul gloried. He gloried in a cross on which not only Christ was crucified, but on which he himself was also crucified. Many glory in a cross on which Christ died, but they are not willing to die on it themselves. Yet this is what God designs. The very blood that atoned for us on the cross has sanctified the cross so that we, in fellowship with our Lord on it, might find the way of life.

Notice how clearly this distinction and this connection between the blood of atonement and the sacrifice of the flesh is taught us in this well-known passage: "Therefore, brethren, having boldness to enter the Holiest by the blood of Jesus, by a new and living way which He consecrated for us, through the veil, that is, His flesh, . . . let us draw near with a true heart . . ." (Heb. 10:19–22). The "new and living way" is not a different thing from "boldness to enter . . . by the blood." It is the way in which Jesus Himself walked, rending the veil of His flesh when He shed His blood, and which, by so doing, He has consecrated for us. This way always passes through the rent veil of the flesh. The crucifixion and sacrifice of the flesh was the way in which the blood was shed. Everyone who obtains a share in that blood is, by that blood, brought into this way. It is the way of the cross. Nothing less than the entire sacrifice of one's self-life is the way to the life of God. The cross with its entire renunciation of self is the only altar on which we can consecrate ourselves to God.

The cross has been sanctified by the blood of Jesus as the

altar on which we may become a sacrifice, holy and acceptable to God.

And now we see the meaning of that phrase which is connected with the altar, and also with the cross: "Whatever touches the altar must ['shall,' A.V.] be holy" (Exod. 29:37). The smallness or unworthiness of the offering of him who brought it did not render it unacceptable to God. The altar, sanctified by blood, had the power to make it holy. And thus when I fear lest my self-sacrifice be not indeed perfect, or lest in my dying to "self" I may not be entirely honest and true, my thoughts must be turned away from myself and fixed on the wonderful power which the blood of Jesus has bestowed on His cross—the power to sanctify all that touches it. The cross—the crucified Jesus—is the power of God when I, by increasing insight into what the cross means, really choose it, and hold it fast. Then there proceeds from the cross, by the Spirit of Jesus, a power of life to take me up and hold me fast that I may live as one who has been crucified.

I may walk each moment in the consciousness of my crucifixion, my entire renunciation of self, because the Spirit of the crucified One makes His cross the death of the self-life and the power of the new life of God that rises out of death. From the cross as a sanctified altar a sanctifying power is exercised over me. From the moment that I trustfully surrender myself to the cross I become a sanctified person—one of God's saints. And in proportion as I believe in the sanctifying power of the cross, and seek to live in fellowship with it, I become partaker of a progressive and increasing holiness. The cross on which I have been crucified with Jesus becomes daily the altar which sanctifies everything that touches it, and sanctifies me also, with a divine sanctification. The altar sanctified by blood sanctifies the gift laid upon it.

But we must now closely consider:

II. The Offerings That Are Sanctified by the Altar.

The altar is sanctified by blood, that in time it may sanctify the gift that is laid upon it. What is the gift which we have to lay on the altar? We find the answer in a word of Paul written to the Romans: "I beseech you therefore, brethren, by the mercies of God, that you present your bodies a living sacrifice, holy, acceptable to God" (Rom. 12:1). The body of the victim was laid upon the altar. Christ bore our sins in His body on the tree. Our bodies are the sacrifices which we have to present to God on the altar. The body has many members, and is a wonderful union of several powers. Each of these separately, and all together, must be laid on the altar.

The body has a head—we speak of the head with the brains as the seat of understanding. The head with all its thoughts must be laid on the altar. I must consecrate my understanding entirely to the service of God, placing it entirely under His control and direction, to be used by Him; I must be "bringing every thought into captivity to the obedience of Christ" (2 Cor. 10:5).

The head has its members also—the eyes, and mouth, and ears. By the eye I come into touch with the visible world and its attractions. My eyes must be turned away from vanity and be wholly His, to see or not to see, according to His will. By the ear I enter into fellowship with my fellow men. My ears must be consecrated to the Lord, and are not to listen to language or conversation that pleases my flesh; but they are to be attentive to the voices which the Lord sends to me. By my mouth I reveal what is in me—what I think, and seek, and will. By it also I exercise an influence over others. Mouth and tongue and lips must be consecrated so as not to speak except according to the will of God, and to His glory. The eye, the ear, the mouth, the brain—and all abilities and gifts associated with them—must be laid on the altar to be purified and sanctified by the cross.

I must renounce every right to manage them; I must acknowledge my utter sinfulness, and my lack of strength to control or sanctify them. I must believe that He who purchased them will accept their skills and guard them in the fellowship of His cross—because of His entire surrender also of Himself. In that faith I must offer them to God upon the altar. The blood has sanctified the altar and made it the "holy of holies"—and all that touches the altar becomes holy. The act of touching is a living, spiritual, real and, for faith, an ever-enduring thing. The reconciliation of the cross has opened the way for the fellowship of the cross. The blood has sanctified the cross as my altar.

The body has also hands and feet. The hands represent power to work. My handiwork, my business, my service, my possessions must all be placed upon the altar to be sanctified, cleansed from sin and consecrated to God. My feet represent my ways and my walk—the paths I choose, the companionship which I cultivate, and the places which I visit. The feet, sanctified by the altar, cannot any longer go their own way; they have been presented to God to be in all things under His leading, and at His service, and they must be "beautiful" to carry the good news and to bring help to the sorrowful and the lost. With hands and feet bound, the body must be laid upon the altar, not having the least freedom to stir—till He enables the soul to cry out, "I am Your servant; You have loosed my bonds" (Psalm 116:16).

Our Savior hung on the cross, nailed there by the hands and feet. In wonderful spiritual union with Him, hands and feet are crucified with Him; the natural, sinful use of them is condemned, and abides daily under that sentence. But in the sanctifying power of the cross of the living Christ they are free and holy, and fit to work for God.

The body has a heart, the center of life—where the blood, in which the soul dwells, flows in and out. In the heart is the meeting place of all the desires and endeavors of men—of all they will or choose, of love and hatred. The heart of Jesus was pierced on the cross. Everything that flows in or out of our heart must be laid upon the altar. I must renounce the right to seek or will anything after my own wish, to love or hate after my own desire. In the case of Jesus the cross meant: "My will is of no account, the will of God is everything"; "the will of God, cost what it may, must be done, even if it costs My life." In the smallest as well as in the greatest things, God's will must be done. In nothing must my will be done—in everything *God's* will.

That is the writing above the cross which Jesus sanctified as an altar for us. The will is the kingly power of the heart. It is governed by our love or hatred, and by it in turn the whole man is governed. When the will is on the altar—that is, on the cross—the fellowship of the cross will soon extend its power over the whole man. My will, sinful and blind; my will, condemned and freely surrendered to death; my will put to death on the cross; my will in fellowship with Jesus living again, and raised to life again and made free; my will now entirely submitted to His leading and authority—this is the way in which the believing heart comes to understand what it means to be on the cross as on an altar. And the believer experiences that the two seemingly opposed conditions are united in a glorious union: his will bound to the cross, and yet free; his will dead on the cross, and yet alive. And so the truth now first becomes glorious even for him: "I have been crucified with Christ"—"Christ lives in me" and "I live by faith."

Heart and head, hands and feet together form one body. They are united in that wonderful structure of flesh in which the soul has her lodging. It was created at first to be the servant of the soul, to be kept in subjection to the guidance of the spirit. Sin subverted this order. The sensual body then became the seducer or tempter of the soul, and has dragged the spirit down into servitude. The only way for the restoration of the order which God ordained is for the body to be placed upon the altar—the body by the Holy Spirit to be nailed to the cross. The body with its eating and drinking, with its sleeping and working, with its wonderful system of nerves by which the soul comes into contact with the world—the body must go to the altar. The power of the cross of Christ which by the Holy Spirit becomes at once and continuously active must have authority over the entire body; the body, with the soul and spirit dwelling in it, must become a living sacrifice to God. Thus that word of deep significance obtains its fulfillment: "The body is for the Lord, and the Lord for the body" (1 Cor. 6:13).

Beloved Christian, when we gather at the Lord's table—to meet with Him, to receive Him who was sacrificed on the cross for us—what our Lord asks us to do is to offer ourselves to Him and for Him. What will He do for us? He will receive us into the fellowship of His cross, as the most glorious thing He possesses— by which He entered into the glory of the Father. In the statement concerning the altar sanctified by blood so that it may in turn sanctify the gift, He points out the way and the place where we may find Him.

Are you willing to ascend the altar, the place of death? Are you willing to make the cross your abode, the place where you will pass every hour of your life in fellowship with the crucified Jesus? Or does it seem to you to be too hard to surrender yourself, your will, your life so utterly up to death as to bear about daily the dying of the Lord Jesus? I pray you do not think this is too hard for you. It is the only way to a close fellowship with the blessed Jesus; and through Him a free entrance to the eternal Father and His love.

It need not be too difficult for you! In fellowship with Jesus it will become joy and salvation. I urge you, become willing. Let us ascend to the altar to die so that we may live. Or is it your fear that you are not fit to complete such a sacrifice? Listen then to the glorious comfort which the Word of God gives you today:

"The altar sanctifies the gift." Because of a sevenfold reconciliation, even the Old Testament altar had power to sanctify every gift which was laid upon it. "How much more shall the blood of Christ, who through the eternal Spirit offered Himself without spot to God," sanctify the cross as an altar on which the sacrifice of your body may be sanctified!

You have learned about the wonderful power of the precious blood, how it has conquered sin and has opened the way into "the Holiest" *above*, and being sprinkled in that "Most Holy Place," before God, it has made His throne a throne of grace. The very same term used concerning that innermost Holy of Holies is used also of the altar: both are called "most holy." What the blood has accomplished by its wonderful power in the heavenly Holy of Holies, in destroying the authority of sin in God's sight, that also is accomplished at the "most holy" altar on which you are to be offered up. In the Holy of Holies where God dwells, the blood by its wonderful power has perfected everything; in your "holy of holies" where you must dwell—the altar—it works with no less power. Lay yourself down upon that altar. Trust the sanctifying power of the blood communicated to the altar. Believe that the blood and the cross are inseparable from the living Jesus, as High Priest, and from His Spirit as fire, and you will receive the assurance that the sanctifying of the gift by the altar is so divine and powerful that you will reckon upon a victory over all your uncleanness and weakness. Lay yourself down upon the altar which is the altar of consecration and approval. The altar is the place of the blessed presence of God, and dying with Christ leads to a life with Him in the love of the Father.

It has sometimes been said that as Jesus is Priest and Offering, He must also be the Altar. There is a truth in this representation. The cross exists not apart from the crucified Christ. At the cross the living Christ is found. If this representation helps your faith, take the crucified Christ as your altar, and lay down your body with all that it contains—with all the life that dwells in it—on Him, before the Father. Then you are a living, holy sacrifice, acceptable to God. Then you will reach the full fellowship of which the Lord's Supper is the type.

"The bread which we break, is it not the fellowship of the body of Christ? The cup which we drink, is it not the fellowship of the blood of Christ?" Full fellowship with the crucified flesh and the shed blood is what He desires to give us. This fellowship is found when we give ourselves over entirely to die as He died, so that we may live with Him, the crucified One, when we lay ourselves on the altar, giving up ourselves to the cross to become one by faith with the crucified Jesus.

Brethren, we have an altar; the altar sanctifies the gift. Everything that touches the altar is sanctified. I beseech you by the mercies of God that you present your bodies a living, holy sacrifice, acceptable to God.

6

Faith in the Blood

"Whom God hath set forth to be a propitiation [a reconciling sacrifice] through faith in His blood"—Romans 3:25, A.V.

IN THE course of our inquiry as to what the Scriptures teach concerning the power of the blood of Jesus, it has become clear to us, from many indications, that the truth referring to the blood is the central point of the revelation of God as touching human redemption.

Faith in the blood of Christ is the one thing which makes the doctrines of the holiness and grace of God, of the divine and human nature of Christ, of our deliverance from sin and union with God, intelligible. In the history of the kingdom of God covering the period from the first to the second Paradise, as well as in the experience of each believer, it becomes manifest that we have in the blood of Christ the supreme revelation of the wisdom, the power, and the love of God.

Let us gather up what we have already learned, and endeavor to set forth briefly and clearly its practical importance, taking by way of introduction the words of our text, ". . . through faith in His blood." The Apostle Paul uses these words with special reference to one particular effect of the blood—reconciliation, which, as we have seen, underlies all its other effects; and so these words may be confidently applied to everything that Scripture elsewhere teaches concerning the blood. If we obtain a better understanding and make a fuller inward appropriation of these words, our labor will not be in vain.

May the Lord our God grant us the teaching of His Holy Spirit while we consider:

I. The faith by which we become partakers of the power of the blood.

II. The blood by which faith manifests its power to enjoy the blood-bought blessing.

I. The Faith by Which We Become Partakers of the Power of the Blood.

"Be it unto you according to your faith." We know that this foundation law of the kingdom of grace is applicable to every circumstance of the spiritual life. Faith is a disposition of heart without which God's most glorious blessing is offered to us in vain; but by which, on the other hand, all the fullness of God's grace can be most certainly received and enjoyed. It is therefore of great importance for us to remind ourselves of those things which are necessary for a right exercise of that faith in the precious blood, for only by faith can we press through to the enjoyment of all that the blood has obtained for us. But before considering these things, it must be noted that faith is born from a sense of need.

The great event which moved heaven, earth, and hell—for which the world had to be prepared and for which it had to wait for four thousand years; the results of which will endure forever—the shedding of the blood of the Son of God on the cross—had an unspeakably great object: to bring about the destruction of sin itself and the overturning of its consequences.

Only he who is in agreement with this object, and who seeks to attain it, is capable of entering into the full fellowship of faith in the blessing of that blood. He who desires to be delivered only from the punishment of sin, or from sin as far as it unfits him for heaven, is certainly not in a condition to appropriate by a strong faith what the Word promises through the blood. But when one truly seeks, above everything else, to be cleansed *from sin itself*, and to live in abiding fellowship with a holy God—truly surrendering himself, with a fixed intention of experiencing all that is possible to be experienced in appropriating the power of the blood—he possesses the first requisite of a true faith in it. The deeper the dissatisfaction with what is wrong and deficient in our spiritual lives, the stronger the longing to be really delivered from sin. The more lively the desire to have unbroken intercourse with God in "the Holiest," so much the more is such a person prepared to receive by faith what God promises and will bestow. Oh, if our eyes were only opened to see what God is willing to become to us . . . if wandering and alienation from God became entirely unbearable . . . if the whole soul thirsted and cried out for the living God and His love—then salvation "through faith in His blood" would acquire a new meaning, and a new desire for it would be awakened!

Where the sense of need exists, there are three requisites for a full faith in the blood: a spiritual knowledge of the Word of God; an appropriation of the Word's blessings; and a loving fellowship with the Savior.

A spiritual knowledge of the Word of God. As surely as mere knowledge of the Word by itself profits but little, so surely faith cannot grow and become strong apart from the Word applied by the Holy Spirit. There are many who think that because they have always hoped in the blood as the ground of their salvation there could not be much more for them still to learn about it. They are convinced that they are well acquainted with and hold fast the teachings of the Church, and they do not expect the Word to unlock anything new for them about the blood. They think so because they have so little understanding of what it means to place themselves under the guidance of the Holy Spirit, so that He, by His heavenly teaching, might inspire the well-known words or truths of Scripture with a new or fuller meaning.

They forget that it is only "the anointing" that teaches concerning all things (1 John 2:27), and that "we have received . . . the Spirit who is from God, that we might know the things that have been freely given to us by God" (1 Cor. 2:12).

The believer who desires to understand aright the efficacious and blessed power of the blood must submit entirely to the teaching of the Word through the Holy Spirit, in private. He must understand that the words of God have a much wider meaning than man himself can attach to them; and that the matters on which God speaks have a reality and power and glory of which he himself can form no conception. But the Holy Spirit will teach him to understand these things—not at once, but only as he devotes time and takes trouble to learn.

Believing in the rich, spiritual, living content of each word given by God, the learner must understand that "the blood of the Son of God" is a subject the glory of which God alone knows, and which He alone can reveal. He must believe it is possible that each effect which is ascribed to the blood can be brought about by a manifestation of divine power that is beyond our conception. In this attitude of mind he should take up, and meditate on, first what one portion of Scripture says about the blood and then what another portion says, so that the Holy Spirit may apply to his soul something of its life-giving power. It is only by such a use of the Word, in dependence upon the teaching of the Holy Spirit, that faith can be strengthened so as to recognize and receive what the blood has to bestow.

By this means it will be experienced how necessary it is to devote time to these things. Time must be found for meditation on the Word in private, so that it may sink into the heart. To read a portion, to get hold of a fresh thought, and then to go away in the hope that a blessing will immediately follow, is of little use. The soul must give the revelation time, in silence before God, to get fixed in the heart; otherwise it will be driven away again by the rush of the world. The thought may remain, but there will be no power. Time must be given not merely occasionally, but regularly and persistently. Day after day, perhaps week after week, I must place myself under and give myself up to the divine truth which I desire to appropriate. It can become in reality the possession of my soul only by obtaining a lodging place in, and by becoming part of, my spiritual being. It is thus "faith cometh by the Word of God."

An appropriation of faith's blessings. In addition to a vital knowledge of God's Word is the real activity of faith in appropriating it, or, rather, in surrender leading to its appropriation. Faith is the *ear* which hears and receives the Word of God. It listens attentively to understand what God says. Faith is the *eye* which seeks to place before itself, as an object of vital importance, and in its true perspective, what would otherwise remain only a thought. Faith thus sees the invisible. It observes the things which are not seen, and it has a sure conviction regarding these things. Faith is accustomed to surround itself with, and to dwell in the midst of, those things which the Word leads the understanding to regard as heavenly realities. So it seeks to behold, in spirit, the blood being brought into heaven and sprinkled in front of the throne—and also, by the Spirit, sprinkled upon the soul, with powerful results.

But faith is not only an ear and eye, to ascertain; it is also our *hand* and *mouth,* to receive. What faith hears from the Word, what it in spirit beholds, it appropriates to itself. Faith thus surrenders itself to the impression produced by what is heard, then places itself under the influence of these invisible objects until they have secured for themselves a lodging in the heart, in their heavenly, life-giving power. Faith accepts it as a certainty that what the Word of God says, the power of God is prepared to make objectively real.

Faith knows that when it accepts the Word but has not yet had the longed-for experience, this is only because it is not yet strong enough to become a partaker inwardly of what it has appropriated. It does not permit this in any way to dishearten it, but only devotes itself the more to persevere, till the undivided soul opens itself to receive the blessing. It knows that trust must always be coupled with surrender, and that if there is postponement, it is only till the surrender is complete, and then faith will surely be crowned.

It is not difficult for us to obtain the appropriation of all the blessings of full salvation "through faith in His blood." Of each different word which is used in Scripture concerning the blood— "redemption," "cleansing," "sanctification," "redeemed," "cleansed," "sanctified," "purchased," "brought nigh by the blood"—faith says: "This word contains a heavenly, divine meaning, richer and deeper than I am able to grasp; but God understands it, and the blessing of its heavenly power is mine. God Himself will, by His divine power, make this matter real to me. I dare confidently to reckon on that—that this blessing, in a sense that surpasses all human understanding, is mine. I must simply await God's time. I have only to live after the Spirit, and by Him be led, surrendering myself wholly so that God may take possession of me. He Himself will bring this blessing to me in its full power."

A loving fellowship with the Savior. It is in fellowship with the Lord Jesus Himself that faith can be exercised and strengthened. It is a matter too little understood, that God bestows salvation upon us in no other way than *in*—not just *through*, but *in*—the Savior. The living Jesus is salvation. He who gave and now imparts His blood, He Himself it is in whom we must daily find our life and our salvation. Further, it is only in living, direct fellowship with Him that our faith can increase and triumph.

Many Christians take great pains in endeavoring to reach a life of full faith by earnest association with the Word, or by straining all their powers to believe—and yet they see but little fruit as the result of their efforts. The reason often is that in studying the Word, and in trying to believe, they have not first of all found rest themselves in the love of the Savior. Faith in God is an act of the spiritual life. It is Christ who is our life, and who imparts faith to us. He does this, however, not as an act or gift separate from Himself; but in fellowship with Him one's faith is active. He is "the author and finisher of faith"; those who walk with Him learn from Him to exercise faith, they know not how. In the face of Jesus, the light which leads to "the full assurance of faith" is always found. Truly to gaze upon His face, to sit still at His feet, that the light of His love may shine upon the soul, is a sure way of obtaining a strong faith. He who longs for such a faith in order to come to the knowledge of the full power of the blood needs to practice this fellowship.

The shedding of His blood was the proof of His unspeakable love towards us. "He gave Himself for us, that He might redeem us from every lawless deed and purify for Himself His own special people" (Titus 2:14). His blood is the power by which He takes possession of us for Himself, to sanctify us. All that is necessary for the more powerful operation of the blood in us is that faith in it should become wider, brighter, and stronger. He who longs for such a full faith will find it only—but find it certainly— in fellowship with Jesus. It is His work to impart His blood; it is His work also to increase our faith. Let us give ourselves in undivided surrender to the Lord Jesus in order to walk with Him, for in that walk unbelief will wither.

This undivided surrender, however, is indispensable. True faith always includes entire surrender. To believe with the whole heart means to surrender with the whole heart to that Jesus in whom life and salvation are. The will and the law of the Lord Jesus are inseparable from His person, and from His love; we cannot know nor receive Him without knowing and receiving His will. Obedience is the one sure characteristic of the surrender of faith. Faith that is not coupled with obedience is an imagination, or pretence; it is not a true surrender to Christ.

But the faith in which this true surrender is found presses ever on to a deeper insight into what the blood means, and to the experience of what it can do. The blood is the life-power of such a faith—for by it, it was quickened to an ever more glorious experience of its blessed sufficiency.

II. The Blood by Which Faith Manifests Its Power to Enjoy the Blood-Bought Blessing.

I shall not repeat what has already been said about the different effects of the blood, but I do wish to point out some special characteristics of the way in which the blood accomplishes its work. Faith, however, must first be aroused to recognize and appropriate these facts: the blood makes all things possible; the blood's effects are ever-enduring; and the blood's effects are all-inclusive.

The blood makes all things possible, for it has a divine efficacy. I have several times spoken of the wonderful power which the blood of Jesus manifested immediately after He had shed it. It was by that blood that Jesus, in His holy, triumphal march, broke open the doors of death and hades, and carried its prisoners out with Him. This was so that then, as Conqueror, He might see the doors of heaven thrown open for "the blood," and that He might take possession of the Holy of Holies of God on our behalf. With a similar wonderful power to that which the blood *then* manifested, it works *today*—in making reconciliation for sin, in removing its curse, in opening the Holiest, and in restoring fellowship with God. With the very same power which was then manifested in those supreme things—concerning sin and its authority, concerning God and His law, concerning hell and heaven—with the very same power, the divine blood works now when sprinkled on a single soul.

That its divine efficacy is too little experienced we must confess. But this is because of our unbelief. If it were not for this unbelief, the mere thought of being ransomed and cleansed by the blood of God's own Son would cause our souls to leap for joy, and to overflow with love. Would not every exercise of faith in the blood cause the sense of the favor and nearness of God, the glory of deliverance from the curse and dominion of sin, to flow through the soul?

But, alas, we may hear and think and sing about the blood, yet it exercises almost no influence over us. Even the very thought that the blood always manifests such wonderful divine power seems strange and unreal to many, and so no wonderful work is done in us, because of unbelief.

Our faith must be quickened to expect the all-conquering power of the blood. Even if there does not at once come a change in our feelings, nor any sensation of new blessing, let us begin in perfect quietness to fix our hearts on these truths of God. When the blood is made efficacious through the Spirit, it operates with divine power either for reconciliation, for union with God, or for sanctification. Let us believe, and still believe, and ever keep on believing in the infinite power of the blood. Such faith will not be in vain. Although it may not be in the way or at the time we expected, we shall be brought into a new and deeper experience of salvation "through faith in the blood." Let us but seek with our whole heart to hold fast this truth: what the blood does, it does with a divine power.

The efficacy of the blood is ever-enduring; of this our faith must be assured. We have already seen on what foundation faith is grounded. By the eternal Spirit the blood was once for all offered, and by the eternal High Priest it is administered in the power of an endless life. Yes, the power of the blood is eternally active. There is no single moment in which the blood is not exerting its full power. In the heavenly Holy of Holies where the blood is—before the throne—everything exists in the power of eternity, without cessation or diminution. All activities in the heavenly temple are on our behalf, and the effects are conveyed to us by the Holy Spirit. He is Himself the eternal Spirit, and He has been bestowed on us to make us partakers of all that has been or will be done in the Holiest by our Lord Jesus for us. He is able to make us partakers, in a very efficacious and blessed way, of the unceasing and continuous activities of the blood—which never for one moment cease. If we long to abide always in the full enjoyment of close fellowship with God, whom we serve as priests; if we desire to experience the constant cleansing of our souls from the stains of sin by the blood; if we wish to know the peace, the joy, the power, of the cross of Jesus in the fellowship of His blood —all these things are possible because the eternal, never-ceasing activities which the blood exercises in heaven may be exercised also in our hearts here on earth.

The blessedness of a clear insight into these truths is very great. The general complaint made by believers about their spiritual lives is that they are conscious of their instability. They have a strong desire that the glorious experiences of special hours should be the continuous state of their mind—and it is God's will that it should be so. If you who desire this will only set your heart on something surpassing all that you have hitherto experienced, and fix your attention on the Holy of Holies now opened, and on the unchangeable priesthood of your Lord Jesus, then you will see that the divine provision for your unbroken enjoyment of His fellowship is perfect.

In the morning before you go out to your work, and to meet the distractions of the day, commit yourself to Him who ever remains the same, that He may reveal in you the ever-living activity of His blood, and He will do it. Even during the hours of business, when you can think of nothing else, the blessed results of the sprinkling of the blood and of the nearness of God—the cleansing, and the victory over sin—will be made yours. Our activity of faith must be an abiding thing, but not in the sense that we must anxiously take care to think about it every moment. No, not that; but in such a way that we, from the depths of our souls, cherish a quiet and steadfast confidence that "eternal redemption" has taken possession of us, and holds us fast by its heavenly activity—if only we are trustful. Thank God, we need not fear. Each moment, without ceasing, we may live here below in the enjoyment of the blessing which the blood has procured for us, because the effects of the blood are ever-enduring.

We must believe in the all-embracing, all-penetrating power of the blood. When the Jewish priests were separated to their ministry, the blood was placed upon the tip of the ear, on the thumb of the hand, and on the toe of the foot. Possession was taken of the entire man for God; all his powers were sanctified—his ear to listen to and for God; his hand to work by and for God; his foot to walk with God, and to go out in His service. In the case of the believer today, the precious blood of Christ will exercise a similar authority over every power, to sanctify it for the service of the Lord.

Christians have often had to complain about a divided life: there are certain portions of life or of work which are a hindrance in a walk with God. The only way to obtain deliverance from this is to see that the blood covers everything. "And according to the law almost all things are purged with blood" (Heb. 9:22).

The entire person of the believer, with all his circumstances and affairs, must be brought into the daily "holy of holies."

It is evident that to enjoy such an experience, a most complete surrender to the Lord is necessary. The priest who was marked by blood on the ear, hand, and foot, so that all the activities of these members might be sanctified, had to recognize that he had been separated to the service of God. The believer must give himself up no less wholly to be and live only for Jesus. In each relationship of his life, of his home, of his business, of commercial or political affairs, he must give himself up to be led by the Holy Spirit, to live according to the law of God and for His glory. Then the blood in its reconciling, cleansing and sanctifying power will embrace everything. The peace of God, and the consciousness of His nearness, will, by the power of the heavenly life, reveal itself in all things. He will experience the completeness of his deliverance from the authority of sin, the reality of his liberty to enter upon a walk in the light and love of a holy God. But always on this one condition: everything must be brought into the "holy of holies," and set right there. The whole life must be spent there, for that is where the blood is and where it exercises its power. This, again, is by faith—faith that is absorbed in the contemplation of what the blood has accomplished in the Holy of Holies, and what power it now exercises there; faith that, because of this, maintains on the authority of the Word that all this power can be brought into uninterrupted contact with the personal life.

And then in proportion as the believer learns, in his own experience, how far-reaching the effects of the all-inclusive blood are, his heart will be opened to long for a widespread experience of the power of Christ's blood in the world around him.

"It pleased the Father that in Him all the fullness should dwell, and by Him to reconcile all things to Himself, by Him, whether things on earth or things in heaven, having made peace through the blood of His cross" (Col. 1:19–20). The power of the blood avails for every creature, even for the one who has "counted the blood of the covenant by which he was sanctified a common thing" (Heb. 10:29), and for those who are "denying the Lord who bought them" (2 Pet. 2:1). The experience of what the blood can accomplish for those who believe will teach them to regard their fellow men as living under the tender mercy of God—under redemption, and under the call to salvation through the precious blood. It will fill them with an irresistible impulse to again devote their lives—which were bought by blood and consecrated to God—to bear witness once more to the blood. By word, by gifts, and by prayer they will be fellow workers with God—and the blood will have the honor which belongs to it. "Not with corruptible things like silver or gold, but with the precious blood of Christ," will become for them the hallmark and all-consuming passion of their lives.

A Christian hymn-writer (Miss Frances Ridley Havergal) has testified that the insight into what the blood can do in its ever-cleansing power was the beginning of a new experience in her spiritual life. Some time later she wrote: "I see more and more clearly that it is only by the abiding indwelling of the Holy Spirit that this hidden power of the blood can be revealed and experienced." May our lives also be under the teaching of the Holy Spirit, that He may constantly keep us also in the heavenly blessedness and joy which the blood has procured for us.

7

The Blood of the Lamb

"These are the ones who have come out of the great tribulation, and washed their robes and made them white in the blood of the Lamb."— Revelation 7:14.

WE have already, in our meditations on the precious blood of Christ, several times considered the question as to what it really is that bestows such value on the blood. Scripture has given us an answer from more than one viewpoint. That value was because of the Son's eternal Godhead, His true manhood, His infinite love, His perfect obedience; in all these we find a reason why His blood exercised such an immeasurable power with God and men.

The words quoted above call us to the consideration of this subject from still another side.

The new name given here to the blood, "the blood of the Lamb," invites us to inquire what we are particularly intended to learn from this expression, and what the peculiar characteristics of the blood and its effects are which are revealed to us by it and cannot be learned from any other expression than "the blood of the Lamb."

When our Lord Jesus is called "the Lamb of God" there are two leading thoughts which are bound up with that name. One is that He is the Lamb of God because He was slain as a sacrifice for sin. The other is that He was lamb-like, gentle, and patient.

The first emphasizes the work that He as the Lamb had to accomplish; the second emphasizes the gentleness which characterized Him as Lamb. The first of these views is the more general one, and we have more often had the opportunity of speaking about the value of the blood from that point of view—as, for instance, in the address "The Altar Sanctified by the Blood." The second has too often been lost sight of. Let us on this occasion fix our attention specially on it, in order that we may obtain our share of the rich blessing which is contained in it for us. Taking as our point of view the disposition which inspired our Lord as the Lamb of God, we shall see that it is just this which makes the blood so precious—it is the blood of *the gentle Lamb of God.*

Let us consider what it means that in heaven they praise the blood as "the blood of the Lamb":

    I.   This characteristic bestows upon the blood its value.

   II.   This phrase reveals the nature of redemption.

  III.   This fact assures us of a perfect salvation.

I. The Blood of the Gentle Lamb: This Characteristic Bestows Upon the Blood Its Value.

When Jesus was on earth He said: "Come to Me . . . learn from Me, for I am gentle and lowly in heart, and you will find rest for your souls." He did not mention gentleness as one of several other virtues that were to be learned from Him, but as the one which was His *chief* characteristic—the one that they must learn if they were to find rest for their souls. He who takes the trouble to understand this aright will have a vision of the true inwardness of the work by which our redemption has been obtained.

The Lord came to deliver us from sin. In what does sin really consist? In self-exaltation; in pride. This was the sin of the angels who fell. They were created to find their life in God alone. But they began to view themselves, and the wonderful gifts which

God had bestowed upon them, with pride. They began to consider that their dependence upon God and subjection to Him was a humiliation, a curtailment of their liberty and enjoyment, so they exalted themselves against God, seeking their own glory instead of that of God. That moment they fell into the abyss of destruction. Pride, self-seeking, changed them from angels into demons; cast them from heaven to hell; turned the light and the blessedness of heaven into the darkness and flames of hell.

When God created a new world with man created for it, to repair the destruction wrought by the fall of the angels, Satan came to lead man into the same opposition to God. The temptation which the serpent presented to the woman was intended simply to draw mankind away from subjection to God. Along with the words which Satan whispered into Eve's ear, he breathed into her soul the deadly poison of pride. And since Adam too responded, self-exaltation became in his case also the root of all sin and sorrow. Man's life is made up of self-love, self-will, and self-pleasing. Self, "I," is the idol he serves. Self is a thousand-headed monster which—embodying self-seeking, self-pleasing, self-confidence and self-esteem—is the fruitful mother of all the sin and misery which is to be found in the world.

The authority of Satan is exercised over, and the fire of hell burns in, all that belongs to "self," "I," "pride." The soul becomes consumed with a thirst that can never be quenched.

If the Lord Jesus was to become our true Savior, one thing was most necessary—He must deliver us from ourselves. He must bring about a death to "self," "I," the self-life, and lead us again to live for God, so that we may live "no more to ourselves." "No man lives to himself"—this is the only way by which man can become truly blessed. And there is no other means by which this way can be prepared for us save by the Lord Jesus in His own person opening the path for us, obtaining a new life for us and imparting it to us. Denial of self, self-humiliation, ought to be the chief characteristic of that life and its inner blessedness. In this way God can again take up His rightful place and become our All-in-all.

This is the reason why the Lord Jesus had to come into the world as the Lamb of God. He had to bring back again to earth the meekness and lowliness of heart in which true submission to God is manifested. It was no longer to be found on earth. He brought it from heaven. In heaven He humbled Himself as Son before the Father, that He might be sent as a servant into the world. He humbled Himself to become man. As man He humbled Himself to the death of the cross. As "the Lamb of God" He denied Himself with a heavenly meekness that surpasses all our thoughts, to become a servant of God and man . . . that He might please God and man. This was the disposition which inspired Him and constituted the true nature of His sufferings— which made Him a complete victor over sin. It was as the "Lamb of God" that He took away the sin of the world.

This is what bestows such virtue upon His blood. He inflicted a deadly wound on sin, gaining the victory in His own person. He subjected Himself to the will of God, and through His whole life, under the severest temptations, He sacrificed Himself for the glory of God with a lowliness and patience and meekness which were the delight of the Father and of all the holy angels. He did all this as "the Lamb of God." He crowned all this when He shed His blood as "the Lamb of God" for the reconciliation of sinners, and for the cleansing of our souls. This is why praise is offered in heaven for His blood as "the blood of the Lamb of God." This is why the Father has placed Him "in the center of the throne" as "the Lamb that had been slain." This is why believers, in tender astonishment and love, glorying in "the blood of the Lamb," praise His meekness and lowliness as their greatest joy and their one desire. As "the blood of the Lamb" it possesses virtue and power for complete redemption.

II. This Phrase, "The Blood of the Lamb," Reveals the True Nature of Redemption.

The blood has its value because of the disposition of which it is the token, just as much as its power is manifested in the disposition which it produces. The Lord Jesus came to do in His own person what we could not do, and then to make us, who did not possess it, partakers of the treasure which He had procured. His lowliness is the gift which He brought from heaven; His lowliness is what He wishes to bestow upon us. And as the blood was the manifestation and the result of the divine meekness in Him, so is meekness in us the manifestation and result of our contact with the blood.

Our fellowship in His blood, what is it but fellowship in His death? And His death was only the culmination of His humiliation and sacrifice. It was a proof that there was no other way by which to attain to the fullness of the life of God—resurrection life—save through death. And so the blood—as a fellowship in His death, as a participation in the inner power of His death—calls us to give ourselves over to death through His humiliation and self-sacrifice, as the only way to the life of God. Even a Christian who thinks that he is trusting in the blood may too often give way to pride and self-will and self-exaltation. But if he only really knew that "the blood of the Lamb" is at work in him every moment, in living power, then he would recognize in this fact a decided call—coupled with a supply of power—for him, in the meekness of Christ, to manifest his faith in that blood.

This is a subject upon which the attention of Christians must be much more fixed than is generally the case. We must learn that there is no way to heaven save by lowliness, by entirely dying to our pride, and by living entirely in the lowliness of Jesus.

Pride is from hell: it is the poison of Satan in our blood. Pride must die, or nothing of heaven can live in you. Under the banner of this truth you must surrender yourself to the Spirit of the meek and lowly Lamb, to "the Lamb of God," the victor over all pride.

Each exercise of faith in "the blood of the Lamb," each act of thanksgiving for the love and the blessedness brought to you by it, ought to powerfully encourage you to desire supremely to know and to manifest the humility of "the Lamb of God." All your worship of God from a heart cleansed and saturated by the blood ought to strengthen you in the blessed certainty that where "the blood of the Lamb" is, there He is Himself in His meekness, to sanctify the heart as a temple of God.

We must not only recognize that this meek spirit, which in God's sight is of great value, must be the object of our desire and effort; but we must believe that it is really possible for us to obtain a share in it. Jesus Christ is the Second Adam, who really restores what the first Adam lost. Our pride and self-seeking, everything that self does or produces, all the sorrow that arises from our self-will and self-love, is only a continuation of that first turning away from God, when Adam fell under the authority of Satan. There can be no thought of any redemption or approach to God without an entire turning back to a life of decided dependence, humility, and submission to God. The only way for redemption from the condition of pride is by death: dying to the life of self. The surrender of the self-life to death is necessary to make room for the new life. And there is nothing in the entire universe that can make that death possible for us, and work out a new life in us, save such a heavenly lowliness as "the Lamb of God" brought from heaven, and which He made transferable to us by His death. What He was when He died, such He was when He arose from the dead. As the "Lamb of God" He is the Second Adam, our Head, and He lives to bestow His Spirit upon us.

Yes, by His Spirit the Lamb of God will certainly bestow this meekness and will work it out in the heart of everyone who surrenders his life entirely to the power of the blood. We have already seen that the shedding of the blood was followed by the shedding forth of the Spirit, and that the Spirit and the blood bear witness together; where the blood reaches there also the Spirit is. John saw the Lamb in the center of the throne, standing as if slain, "having seven eyes which are the seven Spirits of God sent out into all the earth" (Rev. 5:6). The Spirit works as the Spirit of the Lamb. He works with a hidden but perfect power, breathing into the heart of His own people that which is the divine glory of the Lamb—His meekness.

Do you desire to understand how these effects of the blood and the Spirit may be experienced? Do you complain that you know but little about them? Do you fear that in you perhaps it may never be possible? You may learn how it is possible if you are a believer that the Spirit is in you, as a seed of God. That seed appears small and dead; its life-power is hidden and not yet active. Begin to esteem that seed of the divine nature. Keep calm, that you may quietly believe that the Spirit is in you. Believe that the gentleness of the Lamb is also in you as a seed, a hidden power of the Spirit. Begin in that faith to pray to God to strengthen you by His Spirit in the inner man. Take any hour of the day— say nine o'clock—when you will (even if it is but for one moment) send up a prayer for the bestowment upon you of your inheritance, the meekness and gentleness of the Lamb. Cultivate the disposition of welcoming everything that calls for or helps you to humility. You may rely upon it that the hitherto hidden seed, the Spirit of Jesus, will open out and spring up in you, and it will become your experience that the blood of the Lamb has brought you into contact with a lowliness which is powerful and blessed beyond all thought.

III. The Blood of the Lamb—The Assurance of a Perfect Salvation.

We would have thought that in calling our Lord "the Lamb,"

this name would have been used only in respect to His humiliation in His earthly life. In Scripture it is most used in reference to His glory in heaven. John saw Him stand, as a Lamb that has been slain, in the center of the throne. The four living creatures, the four-and-twenty elders, and the hosts of heaven praise Him as the Lamb who purchased us unto God by His blood. "Salvation to our God and to the Lamb." It is the Lamb who executes judgment, who conquered Satan and all his power. The Lamb is the Temple and the Lamp of the New Jerusalem. It is from beneath the throne of God and of the Lamb that the river of the water of life flows. In heaven, throughout eternity, the Lamb is exalted. He is the glory and joy of heaven. Eternity will re-echo the song of His praise: "The Lamb that was slain is worthy to receive power and riches and wisdom and strength and honor and glory and blessing."

And why is all this? "You are worthy . . . for You were slain, and have redeemed us to God by Your blood" (Rev. 5:9). It is the blood of the Lamb that bestows this glory upon Him. By His own blood He has entered into the Holy of Holies, and is seated at the right hand of the Majesty in heaven. His blood has accomplished this. Because He humbled Himself to death, therefore God has so highly exalted Him. As "the Lamb of God," meek and lowly of heart, He glorified God even to the pouring out of His life; therefore He is esteemed to be worthy of being praised forever in the song of the universe: "Salvation belongs to our God who sits on the throne, and to the Lamb!" The blood has effected this.

The blood will be effective for us also. All on whom the precious blood has been sprinkled must come to that place where the Lamb is, and where the blood is, where all those who have been bought and cleansed by the blood will honor and praise the Lamb forever. All on whom the precious blood has been sprinkled will come to the place where the Lamb will lead them to the fountains of living water, and He will complete the salvation which He began in them, for they will then obtain their place in the marriage supper of the Lamb and forever worship God where the Lamb is the Temple and the Light. Yes, certainly the blood of the Lamb is the only, but the certain, pledge of a perfect salvation. And that not only in eternity but here on earth, in this life. The more we meditate upon the glory of eternity, and listen with amazement to the worship of the Lamb and contemplate the unspeakable blessedness which He bestows, the more settled will our faith become that the blood which accomplishes such incomprehensible things *there* is able to effect *here also* a heavenly and thought-surpassing power in us.

Yes, the blood of the Lamb that was powerful enough to destroy sin, to open heaven for sinners, and to bring their salvation to such perfection, that blood has surely power to cleanse our hearts, to saturate them, and fill them with all the power and joy which the Lamb on the throne will, even now, pour out upon us.

That blood is powerful to cleanse us from pride, to sanctify us with the holiness of the Lamb—His heavenly gentleness and humility. In Him we see humility crowned by God, and all-conquering gentleness exalted to the throne. He is able to reveal this in our hearts.

The blood of the Lamb: the pledge of a perfect salvation! Oh that we in deep astonishment and worship might let our hearts be filled with this truth. Our faith must take time to nourish itself by the reality of what is revealed to us: the reality of what takes places in heaven today and shall continue forever; the reality also of the powerful activities here on earth which stream forth from the blood every moment. In that faith we must present ourselves before Him who Himself has cleansed us by His blood and made us kings and priests. He Himself will keep alive in us an effective application of the blood. Just as a garment that is to be dyed must be plunged in the liquid which contains the color, and become saturated by it, so the soul that constantly bathes and cleanses itself in the blood of the Lamb becomes entirely saturated with those dispositions which that blood carries and of which it is full. The gentleness and the humility of the Lamb will become the adornment of that soul. He Himself will cause us to experience through the blood, as priests, a living entrance to God: an ever-abiding communion with God. He Himself will bestow on us, as kings, sovereignty and victory through the blood of the Lamb.

Yes, He Himself will make His blood the pledge of a perfect salvation. Oh, that we might only give glory to the blood of the Lamb! Oh, that each day our heart might sing: "In Jesus' blood is power!" Oh, that each day our confidence might be: "The blood that is powerful in heaven is powerful in my heart. The blood that works wonders in heaven works wonders also in my heart. The blood of the Lamb is my life, my song, my joy, my power, my perfect salvation!" For that blood has come forth from His heavenly gentleness and humility; that blood bestows upon me also the heavenly gentleness and humility through which I enter heaven. The blood of the Lamb: we have learned that it is because it is the blood of the *Lamb* that it has such a divine worth and power. It is the Lamb in His gentleness and humility who has redeemed us; it is gentleness and humility which constitute the power, the disposition, the inner nature of redemption. It is in the way of gentleness and humility that He sacrificed His own will and life, and died—and so has received a new life from God.

Learn, I pray you, that here is your way to eternal blessedness. Let each contact with the blood be contact with the Lamb— more particularly, with His gentleness and meekness. Let your faith touch just the hem of His garment, and power will go out from Him. "Self" is our one sin and sorrow; wholly and always denial of self is our only redemption. Fellowship with the death of the Lamb of God is our only entrance into the life that He bestows. If only we knew what a sweet, heavenly, heart-changing power there is in a humility like that of the Lamb of God, which moved Him to give His blood, how this would drive the poison of Satan—selfishness and pride—out of our fallen nature; how this would bestow on us the water of life, to extinguish the fire of our self-seeking! Would we not rather sacrifice everything than fail to possess it in full measure? How we should praise the blood of the Lamb as the revelation, the impartation, and the eternal glory of humility!

8

The Blood-Bought Multitude

A Missionary Message

"And they sang a new song, saying: 'You are worthy to take the scroll, and to open its seals; for You were slain, and have redeemed us to God by Your blood out of every tribe and tongue and people and nation'"—Revelation 5:9.

WHEN we lay our gifts for the work of the Lord upon His altar, it should not be done from mere custom, or without serious thought. Every penny that comes into His treasury has a value corresponding to the intention with which it is offered to Him; only true love to Him and His work transforms our gifts into spiritual offerings. Thus, it would be well for us to learn what God thinks and says about missionary work so we may think and act according to His will.

The work of the missionary is always a work of *faith*—faith which is sure evidence of things man cannot see; it is guided in everything by what is seen or heard in the unseen world. The outstanding value of missionary work lies in the fact that it is a work of faith. It has always been something beyond mere human comprehension, for mere human wisdom cannot understand it and the natural man has no love for it. He cannot imagine how it is possible for a raw heathen to be tamed and renewed by nothing save the message of the love of God in Christ.

The men who in all ages have stood at the head of the great

missionary undertakings have received from heaven, by the Word and Spirit of God, the light and power needed for their work. It was the eye of faith fixed on Jesus as King that opened their hearts to receive His command and His promise, in which they found both the impulse and the courage for their work.

Our text tells us of a vision of things in "the heavenlies" and it sheds the light of eternity upon the work of missions. We hear the song of the redeemed, who are praising the Lamb that He redeemed them to God by His blood. And in their song, that which is mentioned as of prime importance after praise to the Lamb—or rather is one part of that praise—is the fact that they were gathered together out of "every tribe and tongue and nation." This is mentioned in praise of the power which the blood had exercised: there was no tribe or nation which had not its representatives among those redeemed by the blood of the Lamb. And there was no division caused by language or nationality, for every breach had been healed. All were united in one spirit of love, and were as one body before the throne.

What else is that vision but a heavenly revelation of the high calling and glorious result of mission work? Without mission work that vision could not have become fact, nor could that song have been sung. In that song is set forth the divine right of missionary work, and the heavenly supply which empowers it. Every time a friend of missions, one of the people of God, hears the notes of that song, he receives a loud call to fresh courage and renewed consecration, and to fresh joy in the glorious work of gathering together the "great multitude which no man can number."

In these chapters on "the power of the blood," we have hitherto fixed our attention chiefly on its effects in the individual soul. It is right that we should now, for once, inquire into the far-reaching extent and wonderfully powerful effects of His blood in the world.

Missionary work will appear in a new light to us when we see in what relationship it stands to the blood that is so precious to us, and we shall be strengthened to serve the missionary cause if we understand that the power behind it is nothing less than "the power of the blood of Jesus." We shall learn that in order to carry on that work we must ever regard it as a work of faith—a work which receives its recommendation not from what is seen on earth, but from what is heard from heaven.

In order to understand this better, let us consider mission work:

 I. In connection with the difficulties it has to encounter on earth.

 II. In the light that falls upon it from heaven.

I. The Difficulties the Missionary Cause Has to Encounter on Earth.

These have chiefly to do with the field of labor, the laborers, and the fruit of these labors. We shall consider these difficulties especially with an eye on South Africa. Further, in our reflections we shall mention hesitations about the missionary cause which are sometimes found even among well-meaning people.

The mission field. The very element which provided the great heavenly multitude with their glory and joy is, here on earth, one of the greatest hindrances to mission work: the separation between peoples and nations. The judgment upon humanity's sin at Babel—the division of mankind by confusing their language—is a real curse, under which mankind sighs. In the old heathen world, as a result, everyone who did not belong to one's tribe or clan was reckoned as a natural enemy. Even among the peoples of Europe, how much hatred and strife exists, how much contempt and enmity! The difficulty this creates for the gospel cannot easily be conceived.

Sometimes the messenger who brings the gospel has belonged

to a despised or hostile nation. It was no small stumbling block, for instance, that in the extension of the kingdom of Christ, the proud Roman had to receive the gospel from the despised Jew. In the history of the introduction of Christianity into Germany, into Holland, and into Scotland, it is often recorded that the messengers could obtain no entrance because they belonged to a "hostile people." And even in our own day, the reproach of the poor heathen is often directed against the missionary. He may protest, "Your people have taken away the land that belonged to my people. How can I receive your religion?" Or he points out so much that is wrong and disgraceful in those belonging to the people from whom the missionary comes, and says, "Take your message first to your own people! Why do *they* not receive your Jesus?"

Then, further, there is the difficulty that lies on the other side. The people to whom the gospel must be brought are degraded and despised. At many times worldly-wise people have maintained that the heathen must be civilized first, for then only would they be capable of receiving the gospel. When the first German missionary to India, Ziegenbalg, went in 1705, he and his friends were dubbed by a renowned university professor as "fanatics," "unsent apostles." When toward the end of that century, in 1796, the cause of missions was for the first time considered in the General Assembly of the Church of Scotland, the proposal to take part in the movement was thrown out, because it was, they thought, contrary to nature to send the gospel to a people before they became civilized. For many years in Europe, the thought that a Bushman or a Hottentot in his "degraded state" could experience the power of the gospel was considered the greatest absurdity. Only a living faith in the revelation given from heaven, that men from every kindred and tongue and nation have been purchased by the blood, can supply the courage or power to undertake mission work.

The laborers. The laborers furnish no fewer difficulties than the field of labor. When, about a hundred years ago, the missionary spirit was awakened again in Europe, the missionary societies could find but few ministers who had completed their ordinary course of studies who were willing to go out. So they were happy to accept unordained men and women who had a passion for the work, and to send them out after a short course of training. Much criticism was leveled against the folly of expecting that such laborers could succeed in a work so difficult—perhaps impossible to accomplish.

And yet it was men and women of such imperfect training who became heroes of the Cross: men such as William Carey— "the sanctified cobbler," as he was called in derision—and John Williams, and others, who are now recognized by the Church of Christ, where she knows and loves mission work, as the benefactors of humanity and examples of the glory of Christ.

When, later on, it was proved that men of learning and higher training were valued in the movement, then it was asked by some, what need was there for one who labored among uncivilized people to be so learned?—or how could he stoop to the depth wherein the spirit of the degraded heathen lay? The laborers, as seen and judged by the wisdom of this world, could not be believed to be the instruments by which the kingdom of Satan should be overthrown and the way opened for Jesus to be crowned as Conqueror.

There are many other difficulties which appear as we think of the laborers. What criticisms have there not been in South Africa! We remember how often it has been said that if Dr. Phillip and the first men of the London Missionary Society had been in closer touch with the Dutch farming population of South Africa, who were Christians, and also with the masters who possessed slaves, much of the enmity and condemnation of missionary work might have been avoided. Some of us still remember how at the first Missions Conference at Worcester, in 1860, which God so richly blessed, the one thing by which agreement in the spirit of love and joy was almost destroyed was a criticism of our farmers by a German brother; and the reply was that if the missionary had sought to cooperate more with the farmers, interest in the work among the heathen would have increased. At a still later time the same reproach was often heard concerning a number of missionaries, who, from all who knew them, had the highest personal praise given to them—the French missionaries in Basutoland —that more love and fellowship with the Church in the Free State would have helped to win sympathy and support for their Mission.

It is not necessary nor possible to pass judgment here on the amount of truth which may be found in such criticisms. I mention them merely to point out how truly this division between peoples and languages and nations—the diversity which one day will form part of the glory of the great multitude of the redeemed— is here on earth one of the greatest difficulties in the accomplishment of that work. From our point of view of mission work, it is indeed a work of faith. He who will wait till all the laborers are what he would like them to be understands little about "a work of faith"; he who accepts the word of the Lord Jesus, and builds upon it, thanks God for *every* witness who makes the Lord known to the heathen, even though the witness be imperfect.

The fruit. There is still the difficulty arising from the fruit of missions. This includes the more immediate fruit of the work— the converts—and also those people who have received the teaching but have not become real believers.

As to the converts: how often one hears complaints about the imperfection, the lack of trustworthiness or of truth, or the neglect of other duties which should characterize the Christian! It is forgotten that a true conversion does not include, at once, full sanctification. Remember that the Apostle Paul had to give instructions in his epistles about lying, and stealing, and adultery to those whom he addresses as truly regenerated persons, because they had so recently been delivered from heathenism (Eph. 4:20–28; Col. 3:1–10). And even among European Christians today, sometimes among truly pious persons, there remains much to be desired in what concerns truth and honor, love and righteousness. So although we may well sorrow over the failures of those recently converted from heathenism, this ought not to lead to condemnation or discouragement. The Word of God and His grace need time to produce these fruits.

There is, further, the complaint concerning the influence which learning exercises on those who have not been converted. "Knowledge puffs up"; the educated obtain new thoughts about their value as human beings. "They become unfit for service," it is said. A raw heathen is preferred to the Kaffir who has been to school. One such grumbler thinks that the missionary does not sufficiently preach "submission" as a first duty of the colored people; another gives his judgment that the fault is that the education of the Kaffir is not confined to mere reading and writing. "It is desirable that the Bible should be taught, and that the way of salvation should be made plain, but higher education is not for them, and does them only harm." How is it that mission work and our social interests seem to be at times in conflict with one another? What the gospel has done for our forefathers in the awakening of personal worth, of liberty, of progress, it accomplishes also in the colored people; yet out of the fermentation of this yeast more than one difficulty arises.

Truly in the midst of so much which awakens opposition to missions, faith is necessary if we are to continue to be friends of the movement. Faith does not shut her eyes to the difficulties which exist, nor does she wait till they are removed. The command has been heard by her from the King on the throne. She has heard the sound of the song of the redeemed, from every kindred and tongue and nation; she has experienced in her own heart the wonderful power of the blood. In the midst of all hesitation and deficiencies, she rejoices over every laborer who simply proclaims Jesus, and over every soul who begins to learn, even in weakness, to call upon that name.

II. The Light That Falls from Heaven upon Mission Work.

It is in Jesus' blood that faith finds her power. In the song of the great multitude gathered by missionary activity, we hear that it is the blood of the Lamb by which they were redeemed—to which they owe their participation in salvation. Let us consider how that blood is, in truth, the power of the missionary movement. It is that blood alone that bestows the courage, awakens the love, and provides the weapons to which missionaries owe their victory.

The blood bestows the courage to believe. We may well ask whence came the thought into the hearts of weak men and women of daring to attempt such a task as attacking the power of Satan in heathendom, and robbing him of his prey? If the thought had come from great statesmen, or from warriors who had conquered the peoples of the heathen world, or from men of learning who believed in the power of knowledge and civilization, then we might perhaps have understood it. But no—such men were generally the most fierce opponents of the work. The thought was conceived and cherished in the quietness of hidden circles, among those who were of no consideration or influence in the world.

What was it then which gave them the needed courage? It was nothing else than the blood of Christ, and faith in the power of that blood. They saw in the Word of God that God had "set forth Christ to be a propitiation, through faith in His blood"—a propitiation "for the sins of the whole world." They saw that that blood availed for every tribe and tongue and nation. It was granted to them to perceive that the blood had been carried into heaven, and is now set down before the throne as the ransom for the deliverance of souls for whom it had been lawfully paid. They heard the voice of the Father to the Son: "Ask of Me, and I will give You the nations for Your inheritance." They also knew that no power of hell could prevent the Lord Jesus from seeing the fruit of the travail of His soul and being satisfied. Satan was conquered by that shed blood and was cast out of heaven; that blood has power likewise to conquer him on earth, and to deliver his prisoners out of his hand. Yes, by the sprinkling of that blood in heaven the power of sin was forever broken, and all that could hinder the outflowing of the love or blessing of God towards the most unworthy was removed, and the way opened for His people through faith and prayer to obtain heavenly power so that in their weakness they might perform wondrous things. These missionaries knew with certainty that the blood of Jesus Christ, God's Son, was the pledge that men from every people and tongue would bow before Jesus.

The blood awakens the love to act on this belief. We here on earth speak of blood relationship as being the strongest bond which exists. The blood of Jesus awakens the sentiment of a *heavenly* blood relationship, not only among those who are already cleansed but also with those others for whom that blood was shed. The blood of Christ expresses the surrender of love, even to death; it is, therefore, the death of selfishness, and opens the fountain of an eternal love in the heart.

The more deeply the believer lives in the power of the blood of Christ, the more clearly he views mankind, even the heathen, in the light of redemption. That the blood has been shed for the most degraded bestows a value on every man, and forms a band of love which embraces all.

The confidence of faith—that the blood will obtain its recompense out of every tongue and nation—should be followed by a purpose growing from love. I, who myself owe everything to that blood, must bear witness to it, and make it known to those who have not yet heard of it.

That blood is for all—so also for me: in that faith the soul obtains a share in its blessing. That blood is for me—therefore also for all: in that faith, love burns, and sacrifices self to make it known to others. Yes, that blood is the power of mission work, for it is those who live in the full fellowship of that blood who are driven by the love of Christ to carry the tidings to others concerning that glorious portion that belongs to them.

The friends of missions have need of nothing less than love, with its super-earthly power. It is this love alone, brought down to earth, which is able to embrace the wretched ones, and to persevere when all hope seems lost. There are mission fields where God's servants have labored for twenty or thirty years without seeing any fruit for their labor, and supporters of societies in Europe have asked if it did not appear to be God's will not to open a door there—but love of souls enabled them to persevere, and later on a rich and blessed harvest has been reaped.

In spite of all the difficulties among us by which mission work seems at times to be surrounded, the heart that burns with love to Christ refuses to relinquish it. The laborer may be imperfect, and the work evidently gives but a small return at home, while abroad it may appear to the eye of flesh that loss, rather than gain, is the result; but love is not frightened. Souls which have been redeemed by the blood of Christ are so dear to her that she will wrestle on through all difficulties to save those whom she reckons to be of one blood in the Second Adam. It is the blood—that blood which speaks of the love of the Lamb—that is the power of missionary endeavor.

The blood is, at the same time, the weapon used by missionaries in the strife. It is not enough that the believer has courage and love for the work, and power to begin it, and then to persevere with it. Where can he obtain power really to touch the darkened heart, so as to incline and to move it to forsake the gods of its forefathers; to cause it to receive the teaching of the Cross along with the sacrifice of everything that the natural man desires, and to listen to the call for a heavenly and spiritual life? That power the missionary movement finds in the blood of the cross.

That blood is the proof of a love that surpasses all understanding. That blood is the pledge of a reconciliation and pardon just such as the wakened soul needs. That blood brings a peace and a cleansing which breaks the power of sin, and banishes it. The Holy Spirit bears witness along with that blood, as He opens the heart for this love and this redemption. Just as the veil was once rent by that blood, so also now by that blood the thick veil on the most sinful heart is destroyed. For it is the preaching of this grace of God towards the ungodly by which, in the case of thousands of the most degraded idolators, their hearts have been broken and renewed and have become the temple of God.

The history of missions supplies the most touching proofs of this. Thus, we learn that in the beginning of mission work in Greenland the missionaries thought that they must first teach the poor Eskimo about God and His law, about sin and righteousness. They did that for more than twenty years without awakening them out of their deadly carelessness. But on a certain evening a brother read to a single heathen visitor a New Testament portion which he had translated. It was the story of the agony in Gethsemane. "Read that again," said the man. When he had reread it, the Eskimo asked the missionary what it meant. When the missionary began to explain the sufferings and death of God's Son, the heathen's heart was broken. He was immediately enabled to believe, and then followed a glorious work. The blood of the cross had won the victory.

It is more than one hundred years since that occurred. But every mission field supplies proof that what the wisdom of this world cannot do has been done through simple men and women by their message about the blood of the Lamb. And it is because there are thousands of God's children who heartily believe this, that they will not allow themselves by any means to be turned away from their love for the glorious, precious work of missions—that work by which "the multitude which no man can number" is gathered together to sing the new song in praise of the Lamb who redeemed them to God by His blood.

Beloved Christians, there is one question that presses itself upon all of us who profess to be redeemed by the blood of Jesus. The question is, "What is the value of that blood to us?"

Is it of sufficient value to us to lead us to offer ourselves as a sacrifice to the love which caused it to be shed, and to bear witness to it? Is it indeed to us the most glorious thing in heaven or on earth, so that we have surrendered everything for it in order that the precious blood may have its full authority over the whole earth? Is it worth so much to us that we long that every creature on earth should know about it, and obtain a share in it? Is it worth so much to us that mission work, by which alone the unnumbered multitude redeemed by that blood can be gathered together to sing the praises of the Lamb and to satisfy His love . . . is Jesus' shed blood worth enough to us that in us the missionary movement has true, warm, praying, helpful friends?

Oh, that it may be so! In spite of all its deficiencies, mission work is God's work. Already God has done great things through it. In South Africa there are those redeemed out of heathenism who have lived to truly honor our Lord, and who have had testimony borne that they pleased God. Do not, I pray you, allow yourselves to be led astray by the talk of those who judge it by the eye of the flesh, or in the light of time—the mere interests of time.

He who does not love Jesus cannot understand mission work, for he knows nothing about the secret blessings of missions and the redemption of souls. Mission work is the work of eternity: therefore it is a work of faith. Just as the Lord Jesus Himself was despised when He was upon earth, and not esteemed, yet the glory of God was in Him, so also is it with mission work. God is with it—He is *in* it! Do not allow yourselves to be misled by its outward weakness and deficiencies to misunderstand it. Live for it; give to it; work for it; speak for it; pray for it! If you are a Christian, be also a friend of missions. He who knows the power of the blood in his own heart cannot be anything but a friend of missions. I beg you—by the blood of the Lamb, by your hope of one day joining in the song of the Lamb, by your hope of being welcomed by the unnumbered multitude as a companion in redemption—live as one of the witnesses to the blood of Jesus. As you live only *by* the blood, live also only *for* the blood, and give yourself no rest till all Christ's purchased ones know of His glory.

9

The Sprinkling of Blood
and the Trinity

"Peter, an apostle of Jesus Christ, to . . . the elect according to the foreknowledge of God the Father, through sanctification of the Spirit, unto obedience and the sprinkling of the blood of Jesus Christ: Grace unto you, and peace be multiplied"—1 Peter 1:1–2, A.V.

THE Tri-unity of the Godhead is often considered as merely a matter of doctrine, and having no close relationship to the Christian life.

This is not the view of the New Testament when it describes the work of redemption, or when it portrays the life of God. In the Epistles the three Persons are constantly named together, so that in each activity of grace all three together have a share in it. God is triune; but in everything that He does, and at all times, the Three are One. This is in entire agreement with what we see in nature. A trinity is found in everything. There is the hidden, inner nature; the outward form; and the effect. It is not otherwise in the Godhead. The Father is the eternal being—I AM—the hidden foundation of all things, the fountain of all life. The Son is the outward form, the express image, the revelation of God. The Spirit is the executive power of the Godhead. The nature of the hidden unity is revealed and made known in the Son, and that is imparted to us and is experienced by us through the

agency of the Spirit. In all Their activities the Three are inseparably One.

Everything is *of* the Father, everything is *in* the Son, everything is *through* the Spirit.

In the words of our text, which Peter writes to believers to
whom also he sends his greetings, we find the relationship in
which each redeemed one stands to the three Persons of the
Godhead clearly set forth:

Believers are elect *"according to the foreknowledge of God."*
The source of our redemption is in the counsel of God.

Believers are elect *"through sanctification of the Spirit."* The
entire carrying out of the counsel of God is through the Holy
Spirit, including sanctification—the impartation of divine holiness, which He works.

Believers are elect *"unto obedience and the sprinkling of the
blood of Jesus Christ."* The final purpose of God is the restoration
of man to a state where the will of God will be done on earth as
it is done in heaven, and where everything will redound to the
glory of the free grace which has been revealed so gloriously in
the death and blood of the Son of God.

The place which "the sprinkling of blood" here takes is most
remarkable. It is mentioned last, as the great final end: this is—in
accord with the foreknowledge of the Father and the sanctifying
work of the Holy Spirit—for the purpose of obedience to Christ.

In order that we may understand its place and worth in redemption, let us consider it in the light of:

   I. The glorious purpose of the Triune God.
   II. The mighty power by which that purpose was attained.
   III. The counsel in which everything originated.

I. The Glorious Purpose of the Triune God.

Christians are described as "elect ... unto obedience and the
sprinkling of the blood of Jesus Christ." In the Holy Trinity, the

place occupied by the Lord Jesus is characterized by the name which He bore as "the only-begotten Son of God." He and the Spirit are literally and really the only Ones with whom God the Father can or will have anything to do. As the Son, Christ is the mediator through whom God worked in creation, and by whom the creature can draw near to God. God the Father dwells in the hidden and unapproachable light of a consuming fire; Christ is the Light of Lights, the light in which we can view and enjoy the Deity. And the eternal election of God can have no higher purpose than to give us a share in Christ, and through Him an approach to the Father Himself.

Because of sin there was no possibility for man again to be brought near to God except through reconciliation by means of the sprinkling of the blood of Christ. Scripture speaks of Him as "the Lamb slain before the foundation of the world." It is stated that we are elected to "the sprinkling of the blood of Jesus Christ," which means that God ever and always saw that the only way by which salvation could be made possible for us—the only means by which the door of heaven could be opened for us, and the right and fitness procured for us to obtain a share in all the blessings of His love—was by the sprinkling of the blood. And it tells us further that when the blood occupies the place in our eyes and hearts that it occupies in the eye and heart of God, we shall then certainly enter into the full enjoyment of what He has acquired for us by it.

What these blessings are is clearly revealed to us in the Word of God. "You who once were far off have been made near by the blood." "We have liberty to enter into the most holy place through the blood." "He has cleansed us from our sins by His blood." "How much more shall the blood of Christ purge your conscience to serve the living God." "The blood of Jesus Christ cleanses from all sin." Many such statements show us that our cleansing and fitness to draw near to God—a true and living entrance into fellowship with Him—is the blessed effect of "the sprinkling of blood" on our heart and conscience. In the depths of eternity that blood of sprinkling was the object of the unspeakable good pleasure of the Father, as the means of the redemption of His elect. Is it not obvious that when that blood becomes the good pleasure and joy of a sinner, and he seeks life and salvation in that blood, then the heart of God and the heart of the sinner meet one another, and an inner agreement and fellowship, which nothing can break, is found in that blood? The Father has elected us to the sprinkling of the blood, that we may heartily accept of it and find our entire salvation in it.

There is still another word to consider: elect "unto obedience" and the sprinkling of the blood of Jesus Christ. Here the two sides of the life of grace are placed together for us in a most striking way. In "the sprinkling of blood" we learn what Christ has done *for* and *to* us; in "obedience" we have what is expected *from* us. The creature can have no other blessedness than that found in the will of God, and in the doing of it as it is done in heaven. The Fall was simply the turning away of man from God's will, to do his own will. Jesus came to alter this, and to bring us again into obedience; and God lets us know that He, in His eternal choice, had these two things in view: "obedience" and "the sprinkling of the blood." The placing together of these two phrases teaches us the very important lesson that obedience and the sprinkling of blood are inseparably united. It was so with the Lord Jesus. Apart from His obedience the shedding of His blood would have been of no value. The blood is the life; life consists of disposition and will. The power of Jesus' blood lies wholly in this, that He offered Himself without spot to God, to do His will, subjecting His own will utterly to the will of the Father. "He became obedient to the point of death, . . . *therefore* God has highly exalted Him." He who receives the blood of Jesus receives with it, as his life, His disposition of utter obedience to God. "Obedience" and "the sprinkling of the blood" are inseparably bound together. The disposition manifested by Christ in the shedding of His blood must become the disposition of those on whom it has been sprinkled.

He who desires to have the benefit of the blood must first submit himself to an obedience of faith, which will come to characterize his whole life. He must understand that "the blood" is constantly crying: "God's will must be done, even to death." He who truly experiences the power of the blood of Jesus will manifest it by a life of obedience. In the heart of God, in the life and death of Christ, in the heart and life of the true Christian, these two things will always go together.

If any Christian asks why it is that he enjoys so little of the peace and cleansing of the blood, he may be almost certain that the reason is that he has not fully surrendered himself to be obedient. If anyone asks how he may obtain the full enjoyment of the power of the blood, the reply may be: "Set yourself resolutely to obey God. Let your motto be: 'My will in nothing—God's will in everything.' That is what the blood of your Redeemer teaches you." Do not separate what God from the beginning has joined together—obedience and the sprinkling of the blood— and you will thus be led into the fullness of blessing. From eternity God has elected you to both obedience and the sprinkling of the blood.

It may be that you shrink from this demand. Such obedience seems to you to be out of your reach, and as you hear about the power and blessedness obtainable by the sprinkling of the cleansing blood, even that seems to you to be out of reach. Do not be discouraged, but attend to what has yet to be said.

II. The Mighty Power by Which That Purpose Was Attained.

The Holy Spirit is the great power of God. In the Holy Trinity He proceeds from the Father and the Son. He, by His omnipotent but hidden activity, executes the divine purpose; He reveals and makes known the Father and the Son. In the New Testament the word "Holy" is applied to Him more often than to the Father or the Son, and He is almost always called "the Holy Spirit" because it is *He* who from the inward being of God transfers holiness to the redeemed.

The life of God is where His holiness dwells. Where the Holy Spirit imparts the life of God, there He imparts and maintains the holiness of God, and thus He is also called the Spirit of sanctification. So the text says that we are "elect unto obedience and the sprinkling of the blood of Jesus Christ by the sanctification of the Spirit." It is committed to the Holy Spirit by His holy power to watch over us, and to fulfill God's purpose in us. We have been elected, through the sanctifying work of the Spirit, to be obedient.

The Spirit of sanctification and obedience: these two principles go together in the purpose of God. Here we have also a solution to the difficulty already mentioned, that it is not possible for us to render the obedience that God demands. Because God knew this much better than we do, He has made provision for it. He bestows upon us the Spirit who sanctifies, who so renews our heart and inward nature and fills us with His holy and heavenly power that it becomes really possible for us to be obedient. The one needful thing is that we should recognize and trust in the indwelling of the Holy Spirit, and follow His leading.

His inward activity is so gentle and hidden. He unites Himself so entirely with us and our endeavors that we usually imagine that it is our own thinking or willing, when He has already been the hidden Worker. Through this disregard of Him we cannot believe that when we have a conviction of sin, or a willingness to obey (both the result of His inward activity), that He has also power to perfect that work in us. Let the person who really desires to be obedient, therefore, be persistently and quietly careful to maintain this attitude of trustful confidence: "The Spirit of God is in me"; and let him bow reverently before God with the prayer that He would "strengthen him with His Spirit, by power in the inner man" (Eph. 3:16).

The "sanctification of the Spirit" supplies the power which enables us to be obedient, and through this we also experience what the sprinkling of the blood means and imparts.

This is the reason why so many of God's people have to complain that after all they have learned, and heard, and thought, and believed about the blood, they experience so little of its power. This is not to be wondered at, for that learning, and hearing, and thinking, and believing is, in a great part, only a work of the understanding. And even when prayer is made for the Holy Spirit, it is all in expectation that He will give us clearer *ideas* of the truth. No—this is not the way. The Spirit dwells in the *heart*: it is there He desires to do His first and greatest work. The heart must first be made right, and then the understanding will lay hold of the truth not merely as a mental idea, but as a vital and continuing element within his Christian life. We are chosen in sanctification of the Spirit—not in the activities of the understanding—to the sprinkling of the blood.

Everyone who desires to know the power of the blood of Jesus must remember that the Spirit and the blood bear witness together. It was by the shedding of the blood, and by the sprinkling of that blood before the Father in heaven, that the Spirit was free to come and dwell among us and in us. It was in order to assure the hearts of the early disciples concerning the glorious and powerful effect of the blood in heaven—that it had opened up a free and bold entrance to God—that the Holy Spirit was sent into their hearts. And it was meant to make them partakers of the blessedness and power of the heavenly life that was now their portion. The first Pentecost, in all its power and blessing, is our portion also—our inheritance. Would that we might cease to seek in our own strength the salvation and blessings purchased for us by the blood. Would that we began to live as those who have been led, in sanctification by the Spirit, into the full experience of what the blood can do. We would then have, as never before, a real entrance into an eternal abiding-place near God, and true fellowship with Him. We would know what it is to have a conscience cleansed by the blood, to have "no more consciousness of sins," to have the heart entirely cleansed from a guilty conscience—and thus have liberty for an abiding communion with God. The Holy Spirit is able, in a moment, as we commit ourselves to His leading, to bring us into that relationship with Him in which we shall expect everything from Him.

We have seen what is the work of the Son, and of the Spirit; let us now ascend to see the place which the Father occupies.

III. The Counsel in Which Everything Originated.

Peter writes to "the elect according to the foreknowledge of God the Father, through sanctification of the Spirit, unto obedience and the sprinkling of the blood of Jesus Christ." The counsel of the Father is the origin of everything, in the Godhead as well as in the work of redemption. In the Godhead the Son proceeds from the Father, and the Spirit from the Father and the Son. The whole counsel of redemption is also solely "according to the purpose of Him who works all things according to the counsel of His will" (Eph. 1:11). From the greatest—the ordering of the work of the Son and of the Holy Spirit—to the least—the conclusion of each dispensation in the history of His kingdom, with all occurrences in it and the choice of those who will obtain a share in it—all this is the work of the Father. Sanctification by the Spirit, obedience, and the sprinkling of the blood—this is the portion of the elect according to the foreknowledge of the Father.

Scripture, without contradiction, teaches an eternal election.

That this teaching happens to be strongly opposed is because it is a divine mystery beyond human comprehension. That it has an *appearance* of unrighteousness can be admitted. That it leads to conclusions which seem strange and terrible to our understanding, we do not deny. To comprehend it, man would need the omniscience and the wisdom of Him who sits upon the throne. And to arrogantly take our place on the throne, and give our judgment regarding the eternal destiny of mankind—may we be preserved from that! Our place is at the footstool of the throne, in deepest reverence, believing what God says and adoring Him whose doings surpass all our thoughts.

Our text calls us not to reason about these hidden mysteries, but to rejoice, if we are believers, in what is revealed to us in it, and to make a practical use of it. And then this truth calls us to take special notice of the sure ground in which our expectation of salvation is rooted. The sprinkling of the blood with the obedience which accompanies it, and the sanctifying work of the Spirit by which both of these reach their full authority over us— all these things are from God.

You may, with the most entire confidence, reckon that He who has thought out this wonderful counsel so fully and has gloriously carried it out with the sprinkling of the blood in heaven and the sending of the Spirit from heaven, will just as surely and gloriously carry it out in your soul. This is the right use of the doctrine of predestination—leading you to cast yourself down before God, and to acknowledge that from Him, and through Him, and to Him are all things; and to expect everything from Him alone. Take your place before God, my fellow believer, in deep reverence and complete dependence. Do not imagine that since God now has revealed Himself in Christ and by the Spirit, that you, by making use of what you have learned from this revelation, can somehow work out your own salvation. Let it not be thought of! *God* must work in you to will and to do, before *you* can work it out. God must work in you by the *Spirit*, and by Him must reveal *Christ* in you. Give *God* the glory, and let the fullest dependence upon Him be the keynote of your life of faith! If *God* does not do everything in you, all is in vain. If you expect anything from yourself, you will receive nothing; if you expect all from *God*, God *will* do everything in you. Let your expectation be from God alone.

Apply this to all upon which we have been meditating concerning obedience. "Elect unto obedience": how certain then it is that obedience is indispensable, that it is possible, and that in it lies the salvation of God. The Son was obedient unto death. But this was because He had said: "The Son can do nothing of Himself." He submitted Himself to the Father in order that *He* might do everything in Him. Let every desire to do the will of God, and every fear of your own weakness, drive you to Him who has elected you to obedience. Predestined to obedience: that gives assurance that you can be obedient. God Himself will accomplish His purpose in you. Become nothing before Him; He will become all.

Apply it especially to the blessed "sprinkling of the blood" of Jesus Christ. It was this that led us to the choice of this text. Your heart is longing with great desire—is it not?—to live every day under the clear consciousness which rejoices, "I have been sprinkled with the eternal, precious, divine blood of the Lamb." Your heart longs after all the blessed effects of that blood: redemption, pardon, peace, cleansing, sanctification, drawing near to God, joy, victory—all of which come through the blood. Your heart longs to experience constantly these blessings in full measure. Cast fear aside—you have been elected by God to the sprinkling of the blood of Christ Jesus; you must steadfastly rely on the fact that God, as God, will bestow this upon you. Wait continually upon Him in patience of soul, and confidently expect it. He "works all things according to the counsel of His own will"; He Himself will surely work it out in you.

Apply this also to the sanctification produced by the Spirit. He is the link that binds together the middle and the end; His is the power that brings together the eternal purpose of God and a life characterized by obedience and the sprinkling of the cleansing blood. Do you feel that this is the one thing that you desire and for which you must wait, so that you may inherit the full blessing? Understand that it is God Himself who bestows the Spirit, who works through the Spirit, who will fill you with the Spirit. How can God who elected you "in sanctification of the Spirit" allow you to lack that without which His purpose cannot be carried out? Be confident about this; ask and expect it with utter boldness. It *is* possible to live in the sanctifying power of the Spirit, because it has been designed for you from eternity.

The sprinkling of the blood is the light or revelation of the Trinity—how wonderful and glorious it is! The Father designed the sprinkling of the blood and elected us to it; the Son shed His blood and bestows it from heaven on those who seek in faith; the Spirit who sanctifies makes it our own, with abiding power, and imparts to us all the blessings which He has obtained for us. Blessed sprinkling of the blood!—revelation of the Triune God! May this be our joy and our life each day. Amen.

10

Washed in His Blood

"To Him who loved us and washed us from our sins in His own blood, and has made us kings and priests to His God and Father, to Him be glory and dominion forever and ever. Amen"—Revelation 1:5–6.

THE Apostle John dwelt in spirit before the doors of an open heaven when he was on the isle of Patmos. Time after time he saw in divine visions the glory of God, and of the Lamb, and of the redeemed. Of all the things which he saw, the most wonderful was that which caused the four living creatures, the four-and-twenty elders, the angels, the redeemed, and every creature under heaven to fall down repeatedly in ecstasy and adoration— the vision of the Lamb, looking as having been slain, standing on the central dais of the heavenly throne. And of everything which he heard, that which most deeply impressed him was the frequent mention made in heaven of the blood of the Lamb. In the hymn of praise by the redeemed, he had heard the words: "You are worthy, for You were slain, and have redeemed us to God by Your blood" (Rev. 5:9). And in the reply of the elder to the question to which John could give no answer, he heard this explanation: "These are the ones who . . . have washed their robes and made them white in the blood of the Lamb" (Rev. 7:14).

John had been commanded to describe what he had seen and heard. He begins his book with a greeting (Rev. 1:4–6) similar to those we find in the Epistles—"Grace to you, and peace, from

Him who is, and who was, and who is to come"—the Eternal God. He then mentions the Holy Spirit: ". . . and from the seven Spirits"—alluding to the Spirit in His seven manifestations—"who are before His throne." Then follow these words: ". . . and from Jesus Christ"—as he had seen Him—"the firstborn from the dead, and the ruler over the kings of the earth."

The mention of the name of the Lord filled John's heart with joy and praise, and impressed by what he had heard in heaven, he cried out: "To Him who loved us, and washed us from our sins in His own blood, and has made us kings and priests—to Him be the glory and dominion forever and ever."

It is the blood, and being washed in that blood, which is the central point in his praise. So glorious and so heavenly did this blessing seem to him, coupled as it was with the love from whence it sprang and the salvation into which it leads, that his heart, set on fire with heavenly zeal, just naturally cried out: "To Him be the glory and dominion forever."

We have for some time been meditating upon the blood of Jesus. If there is one thing that befits us, which would be a proof that we have recognized something of the infinite value of that blood, it would be that we also, as we think of it, cry out: "To Him be the glory and dominion forever."

We shall consider John's song of praise. May it be granted to us to see something of what he saw, to feel something of what he felt, to receive something of the fire which inspired him, and to bring something of the offering of praise that he brought.

Let us to that end fix our attention on the place which the blood occupies in this thanksgiving, and inquire what it means that:

 I. He has washed us in His blood.
 II. He has made us kings and priests unto God.
 III. He loved us.
 IV. Glory is to be ascribed to Him forever.

I. He Has Washed Us in His Blood.

We know what the word "washing" means. We wash our bodies to cleanse them from the least defilement that adheres to us. Our clothes are washed to remove every stain or spot. Now, sin is not merely a transgression of the law of God which is reckoned to us as guilt, from which we must obtain acquittal or pardon. Sin has an effect upon our very souls. It is a pollution which cleaves to us. The blood of Jesus procures for us more than pardon for our guilt. When the realization of this has been powerfully brought to our hearts by the Holy Spirit—then at the same time the blood manifests its cleansing efficacy, so that our souls, in the consciousness of the power of a full deliverance from the sense of defilement in God's sight, know that they have been washed whiter than snow.

John speaks of this twofold work of grace in his First Epistle. He writes: "If we confess our sins, He is faithful and just to forgive us our sins and to cleanse us from all unrighteousness." To the same effect he had previously said: "But if we walk in the light as He is in the light"—that is, in the pardoning and sanctifying love of God—"we have fellowship with one another, and the blood of Jesus Christ His Son cleanses us from all sin" (1 John 1:7). This refers to the abiding and uninterrupted cleansing from sin in the case of him who walks in the light, in fellowship with God.

Where does this washing take place, and what is it really that is washed? It is the heart. It is in the deep, hidden, inner life of man that this effect of the blood is experienced. Jesus said: "The kingdom of God is within you."

Sin has penetrated into the heart, and our whole nature has become saturated with it. The blood too must penetrate the heart; as deeply as the power of sin has gone, so deeply must the inner being be cleansed by the blood. We know that when some article of clothing is washed, the water with its cleansing power must soak in as deeply as the stain if it is to be removed. Even so must the blood of Jesus penetrate to the deepest roots of our being: our heart, our entire personality, must be reached by the cleansing power of the blood. "The blood cleanses from all sin." Where sin has reached, there too must the blood follow it; where sin has ruled, there must the blood now rule. The entire heart must be cleansed by the blood. However great may be the depths of the heart, however manifold and lively its activities, the blood is just as wonderful and penetrating in its effects. It is in our hearts that the cleansing by the blood of Jesus must take place.

We are told: "They have washed their robes, and made them white in the blood of the Lamb."

A person's position or character can often be told by his clothing. Royal robes are a sign of royal estate. Filthy or torn garments are a sign of poverty or carelessness. "White robes" indicate a holy character. Thus we read of the Lamb's Bride, "To her it was granted to be arrayed in fine linen, clean and bright, for the fine linen is the righteous acts of the saints" (Rev. 19:8).

The message of the Lord Jesus to the church at Sardis was: "You have a few names even in Sardis who have not defiled their garments; and they shall walk with Me in white, for they are worthy" (Rev. 3:4).

Out of the heart "are the issues of life"—and just in proportion as the heart is cleansed, so the entire life is cleansed. The whole man, inwardly and outwardly, is cleansed by the power of the blood.

How is this washing effected? It is done by our Lord Jesus Himself, "who washed us from our sins in His own blood." The washing began in an act carried out personally in us by our Lord. And He alone can perfect the work. He carries it on in us by the Holy Spirit. Sin had invaded our lives: our powers of thought, will, and feeling were all brought under its authority; and this was not an authority exercised from without, or occasionally, but one which was so united with these powers of ours that they themselves became altogether sinful. But now the Holy Spirit takes possession of the place in which sin had become entrenched. "The Spirit is life," and He becomes the life of our lives. Through Him the Lord Jesus carries on His work in us. Through Him also the blood is constantly applied in its cleansing power.

Our Lord is a High Priest "in the power of an endless life," and thus the cleansing power of the blood of the Son of God is unceasingly conveyed to us. As we wash and cleanse ourselves daily, and are thus refreshed and invigorated, so the Lord bestows upon the soul which trusts in Him the enjoyment of a constant sense of cleansing by the blood. It is He Himself who cleanses us from sin, while we on our part receive the cleansing by faith—by that faith through which at first we received the pardon of sin. But faith's capacity is now enlarged by obtaining a spiritual view of the divine power and continuous activity of the blood. By this insight faith obtains a spiritual understanding, and becomes able to apprehend the fact that just as the blood has had an infinite effect in the Holiest in heaven, so sin has been completely and finally atoned for before God—and that the blood has just as great an efficacy today in the temple of the heart to cleanse it entirely. Faith beholds the Lord Jesus, the great High Priest, living in the heart. He cleanses it in the blood which ever retains its efficacy. Faith has learned that full salvation consists in one thing: Jesus Himself, who has cleansed us by His blood, is our *life*.

II. He Has Made Us Kings and Priests to God.

This is the position for which we are prepared and to which we are exalted by the cleansing of the blood. In this the power of the blood is manifested. If we wish to apprehend aright the spiritual connection between these two positions which are ours through the blood, we must learn it from the experience of the

Lord Jesus Himself.

It was only after He had shed His blood that He was able to enter the Holiest as Priest, and to ascend the throne as King. It was His blood which conquered sin, and by it He was consecrated to enter into the Holiest, into God's presence as Priest. And the blood bestowed on Him the right, as Victor, to rule as King in the glory of God. Such is the heavenly and divine power which the blood possesses.

Now, when the blood comes into contact with us and we by faith recognize its full power, it produces in us also the disposition and fitness to become priests and kings. As long as we think that forgiveness of sins is all that is to be obtained by the blood, we shall neither understand what the office of priest-king means, nor shall we have any desire for it. But when the Holy Spirit teaches and enables us to believe that the blood can accomplish in us also what it accomplished for the Lord Jesus personally, then the heart is opened to receive this glorious truth: the blood opens the way into a kingly priesthood. It was so with the Lord Jesus; it may be so with us also.

Let us no longer be content with standing still at the beginning of things, but let us press on to maturity—into knowledge of the perfection prepared for us in the Lord Jesus: entrance by His power into life in the Holiest; into a fellowship in the life of Jesus, our priestly King and kingly Priest.

What now does it mean that He, when He has cleansed us by His blood, also makes us both kings and priests to His Father? The principal idea attached to the title "king" is that of authority and rule; to the title "priest," that of purity and nearness to God. The blood of Jesus constitutes us priests, and gives us admission into the presence, the love, and the fellowship of God. We are so cleansed by the blood as to be fitted for this. Jesus so fills us with His Spirit that we in Him may truly draw near to God as priests.

The blood of Jesus carries in it so much of His victory over sin and death that it inspires us with the consciousness of His victorious power, and bestows upon us victory over sin and every enemy. He thus makes us kings. Jesus, the living Priest-King on the throne, cannot manifest in us His full power by exercising it from above, or from the outside, but only by indwelling us. When He, the Priest-King, takes up His abode within us, He makes us kings and priests.

Do we wish to know the purpose of this? The answer is not far to seek. Why is Jesus seated as a Priest on the throne of the heavens? It is that man may be blessed, and that God may be glorified in man. As Priest He lives only for others, to bring them near to God. And as King He lives only that He might reveal the kingdom of God in us and through us. He makes us both priests and kings that we might serve the living God; that we might bring others near to Him; that we might be filled with His Spirit so as to be a blessing to others.

As priests, through the motivating power of the blood of Christ, we live for others—praying for them; working among them; teaching them—bringing them to God. To be a priest is no position of idle, self-seeking blessedness. It requires a compelling urge to enter into God's presence on behalf of others. And it bestows the authority and power to pray for blessings, and to receive and carry and distribute them. He makes us kings to complete and perfect our priesthood. It is because of this that the idea of authority stands out so prominently. Jesus fills us with a kingly disposition; He enables us to rule over sin, over the world, over men. In the midst of all circumstances and difficulties, of all opposition or even cruelty, the Christian who yields himself to be made king by Christ lives in the joyous certainty that he is one with Him who has won the victory, and that he in Him is more than conqueror!

III. He Loved Us.

We have spoken of the blood in which Jesus has cleansed us, and of the glory to which He has exalted us. Let us now ascend to the fountainhead from which all this flows out to us—the fact that He loved us. If we desire really to understand the salvation which God bestows upon us—to understand it so that it will tune our voices to sing like that of John, "To Him be glory"—we must first of all understand that its origin and power are in the love of Jesus. Love is the greatest glory of salvation. For as salvation springs from love as its source, so it must also draw us to that love as its object and very nature. Love always suggests a personal, mutual attachment. This is the most wonderful thing in salvation, and it is almost impossible to lay hold of: that the Lord Jesus desires to honor us with His love and His friendship. He wishes to have fellowship with us as His *loved ones*, and to fill and satisfy our hearts with His divine love.

It is John especially who teaches us what this love is. In his Gospel he tells us the Lord Jesus Christ stated that as the Father loved Him, so He also loved us. Our Lord was one with the Father in nature and life. It is difficult for us to form any idea of what that unity is; but love, as the revelation of this unity, helps us in some small measure to understand it.

In love the Father goes out of Himself and communicates Himself to the Son, in whom is His delight and life. He imparts to the Son all He has, and holds communion with Him in a life of giving and receiving. The Father has no such life nor delight nor pleasure apart from the Son. That is the love wherewith Jesus loves His own. He gave Himself for them; imparts Himself to them; lives in them. He wishes to have no life apart from them. From that earliest manifestation of His love, shown in His pitying them and sympathizing with them, He has pressed on to the love which is portrayed by good pleasure and fellowship, striving for a unity in which they would dwell in Him and He in them.

His desire and resting was in them, and hence they learned "with all saints to apprehend something of a love which passes understanding." Only the Holy Spirit can lead the soul personally into that love. "The love of God has been poured out in our hearts by the Holy Spirit who was given to us."

The love of God is such a supernatural, heavenly power that we might seek to make it a matter of deep thought and by that means create some impression in our hearts—but it truly surpasses knowledge. Real participation in it is such a divine matter that none but those who have with great tenderness and wholeheartedness yielded themselves to be led and taught by the Holy Spirit can come to any comprehension of it. The love of God is plainly declared in Scripture to be solely the result of Christ dwelling in the heart. Only where the inner communion with the Lord has become the joy and experience of every day can we know what the Lord meant when He said, "Abide in My love."

"To Him who loved us and washed us from our sins in His own blood, and has made us kings and priests to His God and Father." Let us consider Jesus as He was when as man He suffered and died for us, to give His blood for us. Let us allow Him to reveal in us the meaning and heavenly power of that blood. He will teach us that the most glorious fact in all His work is that the blood is the gift and bearer of His eternal, unceasing love toward us. Let us also think of whither He is carrying us—it is to a full partnership in His Kingly Priesthood and glory. He allows us to enjoy a foretaste of that love which makes us entirely one with Him, and which will live forever in our hearts. Then this will be our first and last thought about Jesus: "Him who loved us."

IV. Glory Is to Be Ascribed to Him Forever.

"To Him be glory and dominion forever and ever." The words of this song of praise are generally applied to God, but our Lord

Jesus Christ is God, and they equally belong to Him. He is worshiped here as our Redeemer. Now at the end of our series of meditations on His blood, and what He has obtained for us by that blood, these words of praise are a suitable expression for the feelings which ought to be ours: "To Him be glory and dominion forever and ever."

These words came from a heart full of the joy of a personal experience of redemption. John writes as one who was living in the full enjoyment of the love of his Lord; as one who both knew and felt in his heart that he was cleansed in the blood; as one who experienced that Jesus had made him a king and a priest. His thanksgiving is that of a celebrant who rejoices with "a joy unspeakable and full of glory"—a joy kindled by the song of heaven to which he had been listening.

Let us take this to *our* heart. Nothing will fit us for taking a real share in this thanksgiving which was offered spontaneously from the depth of John's joyful heart other than a living experience of the love of Jesus, of the power of His blood to cleanse us, and of the kingly priesthood in which He enables us to live. If I would truly attribute glory and power to Jesus, my heart must be inwardly filled with that glory and power. "Out of the abundance of the heart the mouth speaks." Think of how true this was on the day of Pentecost. What was it that moved a band of one hundred and twenty to praise and glorify the Lord? The Holy Spirit, who is the glory and power of the Lord Jesus, had descended upon them; and because they were filled with that glory and power their hearts could ascend in praise to Him, and from them streamed out blessings for others.

It is the glory and power of Jesus to bestow His love on a soul, to effect its cleansing in His own blood, and to appoint such a one to His kingly priesthood. Then the heart overflows spontaneously—"To Him be glory and dominion forever."

You who have accompanied us through God's Word to discover what the glory and power of the blood of Jesus is—ought not your lives and walk every day be full of the notes of praise and worship, "To Him be glory and dominion"?

This is possible. Jesus Himself is the center of this threefold blessing: the love, the blood, and the kingly priesthood. Jesus Himself will so reveal them to us by His Spirit that we shall ceaselessly experience all these blessings.

Let us, as far as our knowledge goes, at every remembrance of His love cry out: "To Him be all the glory." Each time we are convicted that the praise we offer is too weak and too seldom heard, and that it has too little of the joy-note of heaven in it, this may be a help to us if it drives us to seek after such a fullness of blessing as shall make our hearts overflow.

Yes, it is possible. Jesus lives, and Jesus has loved us and has Himself cleansed us in His blood. He bestows upon us the disposition of kingship and priesthood by His indwelling.

It is possible. He can fill our lives with the experience which finds expression in the thanksgiving: "To Him be the glory and dominion."

My brethren, we hope to meet one day amid that multitude who have washed their robes in the blood of the Lamb, and who never weary in singing: "You are worthy, for You have redeemed us to God by Your blood." Let our exercises of preparation for that glory consist in the singing of this song: "To Him who loved us and washed us from our sins in His own blood, and has made us kings and priests to His God and Father, to Him be glory forever and ever. Amen."

This book was produced by CLC Publications. We hope it has been helpful to you in living the Christian life. CLC is a literature mission with ministry in over 50 countries worldwide. If you would like to know more about us, or are interested in opportunities to serve with a faith mission, we invite you to write to:

CLC Publications
P.O. Box 1449
Fort Washington, PA 19034